Hoarding

by Jenny MacKay

LUCENT BOOKS

A part of Gale, Cengage Learning

Detroit • New York • San Francisco • New Haven, Conn • Waterville, Maine • London

LIBRARY OF CONGRESS CATALOGING-IN-PUBLICATION DATA

MacKay, Jenny, 1978-
Hoarding / by Jenny MacKay.
  p. cm. -- (Hot topics)
Includes bibliographical references and index.
ISBN 978-1-4205-0550-4 (hardcover)
1. Compulsive hoarding. I. Title.
RC533.M33 2012
616.85'227--dc23

2012002277

Lucent Books
27500 Drake Rd.
Farmington Hills, MI 48331

ISBN-13: 978-1-4205-0550-4
ISBN-10: 1-4205-0550-5

Printed in the United States of America
1 2 3 4 5 6 7 16 15 14 13 12

CONTENTS

FOREWORD

Young people today are bombarded with information. Aside from traditional sources such as newspapers, television, and the radio, they are inundated with a nearly continuous stream of data from electronic media. They send and receive e-mails and instant messages, read and write online "blogs," participate in chat rooms and forums, and surf the Web for hours. This trend is likely to continue. As Patricia Senn Breivik, the former dean of university libraries at Wayne State University in Detroit, has stated, "Information overload will only increase in the future. By 2020, for example, the available body of information is expected to double every 73 days! How will these students find the information they need in this coming tidal wave of information?"

Ironically, this overabundance of information can actually impede efforts to understand complex issues. Whether the topic is abortion, the death penalty, gay rights, or obesity, the deluge of fact and opinion that floods the print and electronic media is overwhelming. The news media report the results of polls and studies that contradict one another. Cable news shows, talk radio programs, and newspaper editorials promote narrow viewpoints and omit facts that challenge their own political biases. The World Wide Web is an electronic minefield where legitimate scholars compete with the postings of ordinary citizens who may or may not be well-informed or capable of reasoned argument. At times, strongly worded testimonials and opinion pieces both in print and electronic media are presented as factual accounts.

Conflicting quotes and statistics can confuse even the most diligent researchers. A good example of this is the question of whether or not the death penalty deters crime. For instance, one study found that murders decreased by nearly one-third when the death penalty was reinstated in New York in 1995. Death penalty supporters cite this finding to support their argument that the existence of the death penalty deters criminals from committing murder. However, another study found that states without the death penalty have murder rates below the national average. This study is cited by opponents of capital punishment, who reject the claim that the death penalty deters murder. Students need context and clear, informed discussion if they are to think critically and make informed decisions.

The Hot Topics series is designed to help young people wade through the glut of fact, opinion, and rhetoric so that they can think critically about controversial issues. Only by reading and thinking critically will they be able to formulate a viewpoint that is not simply the parroted views of others. Each volume of the series focuses on one of today's most pressing social issues and provides a balanced overview of the topic. Carefully crafted narrative, fully documented primary and secondary source quotes, informative sidebars, and study questions all provide excellent starting points for research and discussion. Full-color photographs and charts enhance all volumes in the series. With its many useful features, the Hot Topics series is a valuable resource for young people struggling to understand the pressing issues of the modern era.

INTRODUCTION

BEHIND CLOSED DOORS: THE HIDDEN PROBLEM OF HOARDING

In July, 2010, neighbors of an elderly couple in Bellingham, Massachusetts, called police after four days had passed and no one inside the home had come out to pick up the newspaper. Police needed a hydraulic wedge to pry a door of the home open wide enough to squeeze inside. The doorways and windows were blocked with belongings—books, empty bins and boxes, and hundreds of other items. Both elderly inhabitants were found dead amid the piles of clutter, the woman's body partially buried beneath a collapsed heap at the bottom of a flight of stairs. Police knocked over mounds of stuff just walking through the home to investigate. The outside of the house, however, was immaculate. Neighbors were shocked to hear that the couple had accumulated so much material inside the home. The homeowner, sixty-two-year-old Susan Abraham, had been a talented and devoted gardener—and by all accounts of neighbors, a very nice person—before dying inside her secret hoard of clutter. "She was a super-good neighbor," said Victor Bowen, who lived next door to Abraham and her longtime live-in companion, Richard Lamphere. "She was the kind of neighbor where if you bought a house you wished she lived on both sides."[1]

The story is one of millions of similar tales of people who seemingly live double lives. They are often personable, kind, generous to outsiders, and seemingly organized people. But inside their homes, where they keep doors closed and curtains drawn, they harbor a secret that grows more alarming year after year—they keep almost everything and throw out almost nothing. In time, a cluttered desktop or closet turns into a room filled with unused things, then eventually an entire house. Piles of items may stretch to the ceiling. There may be no clear space in the kitchen to store or cook food. Bathroom sinks, tubs, and showers may be unusable because they are piled or crammed with stuff. The items making up the mess may be things like empty boxes, bags of clothing, books, newspapers, and craft supplies. Over time, as more stuff is brought into the home and less is removed, the collected materials take over the space.

Hoarders, like the owner of this New York apartment, keep almost everything and throw out almost nothing.

This problem is known as compulsive hoarding, and it afflicts a surprising number of people in America—perhaps 3 to 5 percent or more of the population. Hoarders often hide their habit so well that others are unaware of it, making it a more prevalent issue than many people realize. In recent decades the scientific community has taken an interest in what drives people to hoard. Reality television shows about hoarding have become popular, too, broadcasting an inside look at a usually hidden problem and shedding a new and very public light on the lifestyle of hoarders. A unique branch of hoarding in which people collect dozens or hundreds of animals and keep them at home in often filthy and unhealthy conditions has done much to make hoarding seem shocking, disturbing, and even cruel.

Hoarders very rarely engage in the behavior with the intention of doing harm, however. Instead, they are usually victims of a lifelong habit that has gotten out of hand. Hoarding has been called a mental illness with similarities to obsessive-compulsive disorder, but hoarding behavior is notoriously difficult to understand, even by mental health professionals who specialize in studying it. What is known is that the behavior is deeply rooted in psychology. Some people feel compelled, for various reasons, to acquire items, and they may have a dread of throwing things away. They might have problems organizing information and categorizing belongings. They may have symptoms of attention deficit disorder, too, making it hard for them to focus on tidying up their living space. Some hoarders collect items as a way to cope with emotional trauma they have experienced. There is even a gene that may lead to hoarding and can possibly pass the behavior from one generation to the next. Whatever the cause, overcoming hoarding is rarely as easy as throwing hoarded items away. The problem is not just the hoard, but what makes the person develop the hoard in the first place.

Hoarding habits seem to be a lifelong affliction, and often it takes years or decades for a hoarder's home to get to the point that living there is unsafe. Eventually, though, hoarding begins to have serious consequences. Homes of hoarders may become pest-filled fire hazards that endanger inhabitants and neighbors. Hoarding costs some people their relationships, marriages, and even custody of their children. The legal implications of hoarding are complicated, however, and there are few laws making it illegal, because the behavior itself and the point at which it becomes a hazard or problem are often difficult to define. Ultimately, it is up to the people who hoard to seek help. Many, though, never see their lifestyle as a problem, and they defend their right to live as they choose. Meanwhile, hoarding behavior begins and continues in millions of homes every year, creating an ongoing social and legal controversy.

CHAPTER 1

HOARDING BEHAVIOR, PAST TO PRESENT

On March 21, 1947, the New York City police department responded to a home in the neighborhood of Harlem. They had received a call that one of the home's inhabitants may have died. The community had seen strange things happen in and around the three-story brownstone mansion for decades and had come to call it the Ghost House. Its residents, Langley and Homer Collyer, were two elderly brothers who lived like hermits inside, with no electricity, heat, or phone service. The brothers, if they left home at all, came and went through a second-story window accessed by a ladder. It was the only working entrance or exit. All the other doors and windows were impassable, because the Collyer brothers had barricaded themselves inside their home with their own belongings.

Police that morning had a hard time getting into the house. "After failing to force the front doors, the police unhinged them to find a solid wall of boxes," says New York City journalist William Bryk. "The basement stairs to the first floor were similarly blocked. After forcing a first-floor window, they saw rooms and stairwells jammed with ceiling-high, rat-infested stacks of boxes, paper, and furniture."[2] Hours after arriving, police were finally able to gain entry through a skylight in the roof. What they found inside was overwhelming. Things that the brothers had accumulated for decades filled almost every inch of space in the home, piled to within 2 feet (61cm) of the ceiling in every room and hallway. The house had no working lights, and its doors and windows were blocked by towering piles of stuff, so the place was dark and dingy. A maze of pathways and tunnels wove through the stacks and piles of possessions, and the brothers had constructed booby traps in some of the tunnels so that an intruder unfamiliar with navigating them might trigger a collapse and be buried. There was nowhere in the house to sit or lie down except on the floors of the tunnels. Rats, cockroaches, and feral cats skittered everywhere through the filthy maze.

The Collyer brothers died amid their own mess and brought hoarding to the public eye.

Eventually, police came across the skinny, half-starved body of Homer Collyer, who had died of a heart attack about ten hours before they found him. Homer had been blind for years and depended on his brother, Langley, to bring him food and water. There was no sign of Langley. Police began searching for the missing brother throughout the city as workers started the chore of clearing out the stuff inside the mansion. Cleaning crews had to work from the attic downward, since the piles of belongings on the lower floors were helping to support the massive weight of the upper floors. Working from the bottom up might have caused the house to collapse with the workers still inside.

The event was front-page news. Crowds gathered outside the mansion to see the growing mountain of debris being ejected from doors and windows. When the house was completely cleared weeks later, it had discharged 170 tons (155t) of items, including fourteen grand pianos and a Model T Ford. Langley Collyer's body was also found amid the rubble. He had died ten feet from his brother, apparently after he tripped one of his own booby traps and was buried by his own clutter. Homer probably died soon afterward when Langley could no longer bring him water or food.

After being cleared of its truckloads of trash, the Collyer mansion was in such disrepair that it was uninhabitable. The building was torn down, and in 1965 the lot was made into a park named after the two brothers. A generation of New York children grew up with parents who warned them to clean their rooms lest they end up like Homer and Langley Collyer. Even today New York City's housing law forbids renters to be "Collyer tenants" who fill their apartments with clutter and do not maintain sanitary conditions. The Collyer brothers are one of the most high-profile cases of hoarders in American history.

Hoarding, Uncovered

The Collyers' story captivated New York City. People were both fascinated and horrified by the strange behavior of the two reclusive brothers. The Collyers and their hoarding habits became famous because they lived in a crowded city where neighbors readily noticed their strange behavior and because they died amid their own mess. However, the Collyers were not the only people with a lifetime habit of saving things. Hoarding behavior exists in millions of other homes. It has just been a largely invisible issue through history, in part because hoarders tend to be reclusive and often hide their problem of accumulating too much stuff. Even in the wake of the Collyer case, which brought hoarding behavior into the public eye, it took several decades for scientists to take hoarding seriously. In the 1990s the medical and scientific community finally began actively to study hoarding behavior and publish findings about this condition. What researchers have discovered about hoarding in the past two decades has taken many people by surprise.

Hoarding behavior is far more common and widespread than most scientists realized before the 1990s. As much as 3 to 5 percent of the American population has a problem with hoarding—accumulating more possessions than they can realistically keep or store. This means that anywhere from 6 million to 15 million Americans may be hoarders, and the behavior is not limited by gender, race, ethnicity, or one's economic status. Some people who do not have much money hoard, but so do some people who are financially well off. Hoarders also have varying degrees of education—some never completed high school, but many have college degrees. Hoarding behavior does seem, at first glance, to be age specific—the most severe cases of hoarding occur among people who are middle-aged to elderly—but these people may have been hoarding all their lives and only in later decades accumulated enough stuff to have a problem. More women seem to hoard than men, though either gender can develop the behavior. Hoarding knows few social boundaries. Chances are that almost everybody knows someone who hoards.

One reason why hoarding was not widely studied until the 1990s, despite being a fairly widespread behavior, is that hoarders tend to hide the situation from other people. Many live very typical lives apart from their habit of hoarding. Those who accumulate piles of objects usually do so within their own living spaces. Hiding the issue from others may be as simple as not inviting guests indoors or entertaining visitors. Therefore, friends or even relatives often do not realize when a person's hoarding behavior has become severe. Despite a recent outpouring of interest from the scientific community, hoarding remains a largely hidden behavior.

Peering in at Hoarders

Partly in response to studies that have shown hoarding behavior to be widespread and partly to expose an issue that by its nature is often kept hidden, the media has seized on hoarding as a hot topic in recent years. Reality-television shows like A&E's *Hoarders*, TLC's *Hoarding: Buried Alive*, and Animal Planet's *Confessions: Animal Hoarding* have become popular since 2008, showcasing intimate details of the homes and lives of hoarders, usually those who have taken the behavior to extremes. Shows like these raise awareness of the two main types of hoarding—the accumulation of possessions and the accumulation of pets. The shows have certain things in common, usually including panoramic views of hoarders' cluttered or dirty living spaces followed by close-up camera shots of the most soiled or cluttered areas of the home. Each episode features an individual or family living amid junk piles or a crowd of animals. Psychologists are brought in to help the featured hoarders talk through the behavior on camera. The shows usually try to explain to viewers some of the reasons behind why a person would begin to hoard in the first place.

In episodes of *Hoarders* the featured person or family usually has a short deadline to get stuff cleared out before being evicted from their home or is facing some other punishment. Words appear on a black-and-white screen throughout the episode reminding viewers of what is at stake and how little time remains for the person to clean up his or her home. In episodes of *Hoarding: Buried Alive* and *Confessions: Animal Hoarding*, there is a narrator, and the focus is more on working with the hoarders themselves than on meeting deadlines or facing punishments. Nevertheless, all three programs thrive on the shock factor of showing extreme cases of hoarding, and many viewers watch because they expect to be disgusted by messiness, clutter, and filth.

Such shows have done much to give an inside look at hoarding and its causes. Every episode's featured person or family must agree to let in camera crews and meet with psychologists or other experts. In exchange they receive payment from the show and the offer of free psychological help for their hoarding behavior. However, because they are being paid for participating and because the television networks try to snag viewers by showing only the most shocking conditions and behaviors, these reality shows have also been criticized for deliberately making hoarding behavior look as bad as possible. "I call them 'exploitainment,'" says Debbie Stanley, a licensed counselor who has worked with hoarding clients since 1997. "Overall they tend to highlight examples of low or no insight, such as a client who cannot recognize that a particular food item is rotten, and they zoom in on squalor." Stanley says these shows give viewers the false impression that all hoarders live in filth like what is shown on TV. "In fact," she says, "many hoarding situations are not squalid. Many people who hoard are otherwise high-functioning, and their homes reflect this."[3]

HOARDING THE DRAMA

"You can't change this behavior in TV time; it's a long-term process. But that's not as dramatic as when you've got a burly cleaning crew throwing out someone's prized collection of 10-year-old newspapers."—Randy O. Frost, a leading researcher in the study of hoarding behavior

Quoted in Thomas Rogers. "Stuff: The Psychology of Hoarding." Salon.com, April 25, 2010. www.salon.com/2010/04/25/hoarding_interview_stuff.

Not only might such television shows blow the hoarding problem out of proportion just so the networks can shock viewers and make money, they also give viewers an unrealistic idea that hoarding can be fixed or corrected after a few visits with a psychiatrist and one weekend of throwing things away. "Hoarding does not develop overnight and it will not be 'fixed' in the period of a few days of filming," says Lori Watson, a registered nurse who works with clients who hoard. "The techniques used to assist the families are often less than ideal. . . . Removing the possessions and/or animals over a short period of time (a few

Classifications of Hoarding

In 2003 the National Study Group on Chronic Disorganization created a five-level scale for measuring the severity of clutter inside a person's home. Level I is a home that can still be used and lived in as it was intended; residents may just need advice with organizing their belongings more effectively. A Level II home contains clutter to the point of blocking some windows or exits but is not yet to the point where belongings have overwhelmed the living space. A Level III home has insects or rodents, and walkways are narrowed by clutter. Community organizations and mental health providers are usually recommended at this level to address causes of hoarding. Level IV usually involves psychological, medical, and financial hardship for the client, and construction and pest control specialists usually must get involved to bring the home up to acceptable living standards. Level V on the scale requires community agencies or services to make the house safely livable again, possibly including legal advisors and fire and safety inspectors. This scale gives professionals standard measurements for rating the degree of hoarding, helps them decide what additional resources might be necessary, and allows them to set preferences as to the degree of hoarding behavior with which they are comfortable working.

days) will provoke severe anxiety in those who hoard and can create an even stronger urge to hoard again."[4] Not only might reality TV shows make hoarding behavior worse in the long run for the people they feature, they may affect the general population's approach to hoarding, too. Hoarders who see these shows or hear other people talking about them might become more ashamed of their own living conditions, withdraw even more from friends and other social contacts, and avoid getting help because they fear having their private lives put on display. "These shows can do damage if viewers perceive at the end of the episode that . . . the process is emotionally very traumatic and already strained family relationships are further damaged,"[5] Watson says.

The Benefits of Exposing Hoarding

At the same time, intense media attention has also done much to shed light on hoarding as an issue and even to spur many people to realize they have a problem and seek help. Some hoarders may feel relieved when they see other people on TV who share their same problems or personality traits and who successfully get help for their situation. Television shows about hoarding have raised public awareness and understanding of hoarding, too. In response to these shows, people with family members or friends who have hoarding behavior have started talking to psychology professionals. "The pros to these shows are that they have brought this mental health issue into the light and have shown that there is help available for those that suffer from the effects of the hoarding," says Watson. "Hoarding has been a mental health

Matt Paxton's (pictured) clutter clean-up company was featured on an episode of Hoarders. *Television shows about hoarding have raised public awareness and understanding of hoarding.*

issue that in the past was not discussed openly and was kept hidden within families. [Television] has prompted people to reach out for help for their loved ones who are seriously impacted by the hoarding."[6]

BY PERMISSION ONLY

"I call them on the phone before I get on the show and I introduce myself and tell them one thing, that 'I promise not to throw anything away.' . . . None of the teams get to throw anything away without her or his permission."—Dorothy Breininger, producer of A&E's reality TV series *Hoarders*

Quoted in *Inside Pulse*. "Exclusive Interview, from A&E's 'Hoarders,' Dorothy Breininger." November 15, 2009. http://insidepulse.com/2009/11/15/exclusive-interview-from-aes -hoarders-dorothy-breininger.

Today, in part because of increased media attention to hoarding, there are support groups for hoarders and for their family members. Organizations like the International OCD Foundation provide information and resources that can help hoarders understand the behavior, recognize when it has become a problem in their lives, and do something to improve their living conditions. Psychologists also understand much more about hoarding behaviors now than they did in the past, and increased research on hoarding has led mental health professionals to come up with strategies that help hoarders better understand their own behavior and find positive, effective ways to change it. Thus, although reality TV at times might exploit drastic cases of hoarding in order to make money and get higher television ratings, it also may nudge some individuals who are troubled by their behavior toward positive channels for getting help.

Hoarding as Front-Page News

Hoarding cases featured on television shows are deliberately portrayed as severe and shocking. Not all hoarding cases are as extreme as what is seen on TV. Still, as more people watch these shows, they also become more likely to report suspicions about hoarding problems in their own neighborhoods. When these potential cases of hoarding are investigated by authorities, media coverage of hoarding often shifts from documentary-style reporting to prime-time and front-page news stories. This is particularly true in cases of animal hoarding that have gotten out of hand. Unlike documentaries or reality TV shows, which tend to give featured hoarders an opportunity to explain why they do what they do, media coverage of hoarding cases usually aims instead to inform the public of shocking facts and often results in

News coverage of animal hoarding, like this seizure of more than six hundred cats in Gainesville, Florida, is often considered exploitive and insensitive to the hoarder who probably has a serious psychological issue.

widespread disgust and even anger toward hoarders. News coverage can portray hoarders not just as people with strange habits but as troubled individuals.

One example is a story by NBC Philadelphia about a man whose home was investigated by police in July 2011 after a tip that he was hoarding animals. The news program quoted George Bengal, a spokesperson for the Pennsylvania Society for the Protection of Cruelty to Animals, as saying, "This is an extremely bizarre case. This is a hoarder situation but I think that the individual who lives in here has every kind of species known to man."[7] In reality, while the animals' owner did have a large variety of pets, including iguanas, turtles, cats, roosters, tarantulas, and an alligator, his collection fell far short of *every* species known to man. The story showed how the news media often gather quotes from witnesses and officials that exaggerate hoarding situations and refer to them with judgmental opinions like "extremely bizarre."

Sociologist Arnold Arluke and several of his colleagues say the media try to fit hoarding situations like these into standard reporting methods, such as showing how a crime or a problem was effectively solved by police who had to step in. "Press reports of the private troubles of hoarders, co-dwellers, friends, and neighbors transform these individual experiences into a public issue, as occurs with crime incidents in the news,"[8] they say. Rarely in such news stories are the hoarders themselves interviewed, but when they are, their statements are often spoken in fear, anger, or heartbreak because their homes have just been invaded, and in some cases, raided. Hoarders' statements to the press, often made in a moment of fear or anger, may unfairly make them seem like combative or uncooperative people. Sometimes hoarders are arrested, and news reporting of this fact can make the public think of all hoarders as criminals. Arluke and colleagues say that rarely are hoarders given jail time or other harsh penalties in court, the way dangerous criminals would be. Charges against hoarders are often minor and may even be dismissed in court. But by the time any court follow-up occurs in the reported cases, the media have already moved on to other breaking news. The public often is left to believe that featured hoarders, especially animal hoarders, are criminals who were punished harshly once they were caught. "This may be the sole source of information most people get about this behavior,"[9] say Arluke and colleagues. In this way the media do much to expose the hidden world of hoarding but also to misrepresent it.

A Social Problem or Just a Lifestyle Choice?

Despite media coverage that may portray hoarders as being borderline criminals, there are few actual laws as to how many possessions or items a person can keep in his or her home. People who hoard objects are rarely doing anything in which police or government officials can or should legally intervene. Hoarders

Hoarders typically do not engage in their behavior of accumulating and keeping items for criminal reasons or because they intend to harm someone.

Detecting Hoarders in Literature

Hoarding was not widely studied by doctors and scientists or even scientifically defined as a mental disorder until the 1990s, but it is not a recent phenomenon. For centuries famous authors have included people with hoarding characteristics in their stories. Arthur Conan Doyle's classic fictional detective from the 1800s, Sherlock Holmes, is one famous example. Holmes's friend and roommate, Watson, described him in one story as "one of the most untidy men that ever drove a fellow lodger to distraction." Watson said Holmes had "a horror of destroying documents," though it was only "once in every year or two that he would muster energy to docket and arrange them." In Watson's description Holmes's papers accumulated until every corner of the room was stacked with bundles of manuscripts, and these "could not be put away save by their owner." Holmes's dread of throwing out papers, his reluctance to sort and organize, and his insistence that no one else touch his things are signs that Doyle likely had known a hoarder or two in his lifetime and wrote these traits into the fictional character of Sherlock Holmes.

Arthur Conan Doyle. *The Complete Sherlock Holmes*. Vol. 2. New York: Barnes & Noble Classics, 2003, p. 461.

Arthur Conan Doyle's fictional character Sherlock Holmes, pictured in this illustration, exhibits hoarding characteristics.

typically do not engage in their behavior of accumulating and keeping items or animals for criminal reasons or because they intend to harm anyone. It is difficult, therefore, to determine when or even whether hoarding is a crime. Furthermore, there is even debate within the scientific community as to when collecting items, keeping pets, or creating clutter in the home should even be classified as hoarding, when such behavior becomes a disorder, and what kind of disorder hoarding actually might be. Research and press coverage about hoarding has brought the issue into the public eye in recent decades, but many questions about this behavior remain, even among the scientists who study it.

CHAPTER 2

HOARDING AS A DISORDER

Psychologists and psychiatrists—specialists who diagnose and treat mental, addictive, and emotional disorders—have taken a special interest in hoarding behavior since the 1990s. Their research involves surveying and interviewing people who have a problem with hoarding. They look for patterns and similarities across the group and also for unique traits that may exist among hoarders. These methods help them learn how best to define hoarding behavior, what causes it, and what characteristics hoarders have in common with people who experience other mental or emotional disorders. Psychologists still have much to learn about hoarding, in part because it has traditionally been difficult to find people to study. Some hoarders hide their habit of collecting pets or things, and others do not see their behavior as a problem for which they should seek help.

Television shows and news reports make more people aware of hoarding and may encourage hoarders and their families to seek assistance, so scientists have had more cases of hoarding to study in recent years than ever before. The more they learn about hoarding, however, the more psychology professionals tend to disagree about exactly what psychological conditions it is most related to and whether a hoarder's behavior actually constitutes a disorder. Fully understanding and properly classifying hoarding is essential if scientists are to help people successfully deal with the problem. However, it can be hard to determine when, and even whether, hoarding has become a disorder in the first place.

Psychologists have taken a special interest in hoarding behavior in recent years.

Hoarding Versus Collecting

Millions of Americans may fit the definition of hoarders, although not all of them would agree that they have a problem. The current scientific definition of hoarding is the collecting of—and the inability to throw away—a great number of possessions that have little to no value. Eventually, these possessions take up so much space in the person's home that they cause distress and disrupt his or her life. One problem with this definition is that different people have different ideas about what items have value and are worth keeping. What one person would consider junk, another might find interesting or pretty. Hoarders tend to keep things other people would throw away, such as stacks of fast-food napkins or piles of outdated newspapers and magazines. However, they also may have many costly items, such as jewelry or art, packed in among less valuable things.

Different opinions about what is valuable can make it hard to differentiate hoarding from collecting. Many people do collect things deliberately, such as coins, postage stamps, or baseball cards. Such items may have little or no value to most people, but the collector may find great worth and meaning in them, even if the collection takes up a lot of space in his or her home. Defining hoarding as the collection of *valueless* things, therefore, can make it hard for someone to decide if he or she is a hoarder. Items hoarders collect and keep may seem very valuable to them, and nonhoarders often collect things, too. "Everyone acquires objects," say psychologists Max Taylor and Ethel Quayle. "Acquisition of items," they say, is "neither unusual or inappropriate."[10] This is one reason hoarders often do not see themselves as being different from other people.

A Different View

"You can't look through our eyes and see what the hoarder is seeing. These aren't people who purposefully want to be slobs or a danger to their neighbors. These are people who have a mental health problem."— Bonnie Klem, social worker, Montgomery County, Virginia

Quoted in Leah Fabel. "Local Task Forces Target Dangerous Hoarding." *Washington Examiner*, July 13, 2011. http://washingtonexaminer.com/local/virginia/2011/07/area-task -forces-target-dangerous-hoarding#ixzz1fGW7wz5l.

Psychologists say the difference between hoarding and collecting is that collectors know what items they already have and only seek out new ones that are different from the other things in their collection, such as a rare postage stamp or baseball card. Collectors also tend to keep their items organized, carefully

The Hoarder Psychological Profile

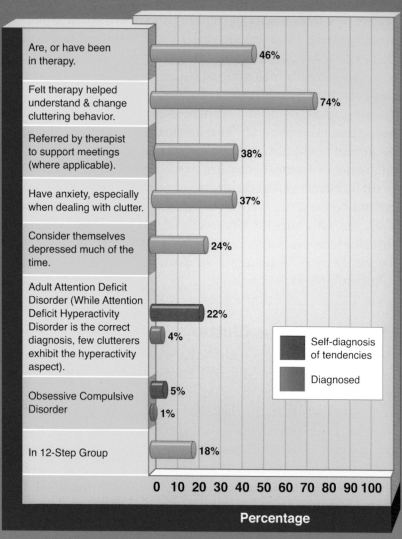

Are, or have been in therapy. **46%**

Felt therapy helped understand & change cluttering behavior. **74%**

Referred by therapist to support meetings (where applicable). **38%**

Have anxiety, especially when dealing with clutter. **37%**

Consider themselves depressed much of the time. **24%**

Adult Attention Deficit Disorder (While Attention Deficit Hyperactivity Disorder is the correct diagnosis, few clutterers exhibit the hyperactivity aspect). **22%** **4%**

Obsessive Compulsive Disorder **5%** **1%**

In 12-Step Group **18%**

Self-diagnosis of tendencies

Diagnosed

0 10 20 30 40 50 60 70 80 90 100

Percentage

classifying and storing them so they can find a particular one at any time. Collectors may display their collections, too, and will show off and describe items with pride if a visitor shows interest. Hoarders, on the other hand, tend to acquire new items even if they have many of the same object already. They often buy or collect new things without thinking about what their collection actually needs. Hoarders are rarely good organizers and usually do not classify collected items to find a particular one easily. Instead, they are likely to put a new item into a pile with unrelated things and may not be able to find it again.

Most hoarders do not display or take pride in their collections, either. More commonly, items are spread throughout the home and could not be easily found even if someone did show an interest in seeing them. Most psychologists agree that the type of things collected and the degree of organization of those things are important traits distinguishing someone who collects from someone who hoards. "The sense of specificity and selectivity that characterizes the collection is missing in the hoard," say Taylor and Quayle. "A house full of clocks or china cats is unlikely to have the same negative impact on the outside observer as a house full of empty cardboard boxes."[11]

Hoarding Versus Clutter

Hoarding usually begins with the habit of haphazardly accumulating and storing things. Hoarders have another important characteristic, too—they resist throwing things away. Almost everyone has keepsakes that represent cherished memories, and if these items were lost or destroyed, it would cause the owner sadness. Hoarders, however, tend to feel this way about *all* their possessions, even things like empty boxes that could be replaced easily. Most hoarders have an emotional attachment to possessions in general. People who hoard "regard their stuff as part of themselves," say Bruce M. Hyman and Cherry Pedrick, mental health professionals who specialize in treating hoarding and other compulsive behavior. "They attach more sentiment to objects than nonhoarders do, and they find an extreme degree of emotional comfort in their possessions."[12] Hoarders may feel great sorrow or regret about throwing things away, so they tend to avoid doing so.

The result of never discarding anything is that possessions begin to build up in a person's home. Many people have cluttered or messy areas and may put off cleaning these spaces, but hoarders differ in an important way—they emotionally dread cleaning up, not because it will take time but because it means parting with

Many people have cluttered or messy areas and may put off cleaning these spaces, but hoarders differ in an important way—they emotionally dread cleaning up.

some of their things. Someone who has merely put off house-work for a while can easily sort through clutter and throw out unused or unimportant items. Most people feel better when a cluttered or messy room is finally clean. For hoarders, though, throwing things away brings regret, not relief. "At times, the person who hoards does discard a possession, but doubts about the decision creep in and she soon retrieves the item from the trash," say psychologists Michael A. Tompkins and Tamara L. Hartl. Hoarders have even been known to go to the dump to look for something that they are sorry they threw away. "In choosing to save everything," say Tompkins and Hartl, "the person can prevent the possibility of regretting a decision to throw something away. . . . By avoiding discarding anything, they avoid reexperiencing intense feelings of grief and loss."[13] Most hoarders feel emotionally unable to get rid of clutter.

Unlivable Homes

Eventually, the habits of acquiring new things and not getting rid of older things will overwhelm a person's home. There is only so much space in a house or an apartment, and eventually, hoarders fill that space with their belongings. Piles and stacks of items cover the floor and the furniture. In time, there may be no comfortable place left to sit or sleep. Even the kitchen and bathrooms may become unusable. Sinks, countertops, stoves, and refrigerators may be covered or filled with things, and belongings may even be stacked in bathtubs or showers so that these spaces cannot be used for hygiene. A hoarder often forges paths through the piles just to get from one room to another. At this point, hoarding behavior can cause considerable stress. The home is unlivable, but the person may be overwhelmed or depressed by the idea of doing anything about it.

Being overtaken by one's belongings is what makes hoarders different from collectors, nostalgic people, and those who are merely untidy. "The passion of a collector, the procrastination of someone who hasn't taken the time to put things away, the sentimentality of one who saves reminders of important personal events—all these are part of the hoarding story," say psychologists and hoarding researchers Randy O. Frost and Gail Steketee. "We all become attached to our possessions and save things other people wouldn't. So we all share some of the hoarding orientation." However, they note, "the boundaries between normal and not normal blur when it comes to hoarding."[14] When people can no longer live normally in their homes but cannot bring themselves to do anything about it, this is generally when psychologists classify hoarding behavior as a mental disorder called a compulsion.

Compulsion to Keep

A compulsion is an intense, even irresistible urge to engage in a certain behavior. All people have certain compulsions, such as the urge to eat when hungry or drink when thirsty. For some people, though, compulsive behaviors go beyond natural instincts. These people may feel convinced that their very lives depend on performing certain behaviors that are not actually related to survival. This is when a compulsion becomes a disorder.

HANDS OFF

"I really want to deal with it. There are days when I feel it wouldn't matter if I got rid of everything, but the moment passes, and I hate the idea of people touching my things. I worry and begin to panic."—Vasoulla Harman, hoarder

Quoted in Nikki Murfitt. "'My Mother Is a Hoardaholic . . . and Yes That IS a Real Condition,' Says TV Star Jasmine Harman." *Daily Mail* (London), August 13, 2011. www.daily mail.co.uk/health/article-2025643/Jasmine-Harmin-My-mother-hoardaholic—yes-IS-real -condition.html#ixzz1fGURG2aN.

Most compulsive disorders begin with an obsession—a recurring concern that a person cannot get out of his or her head. Obsessions are rarely rational. They may involve an intense worry of touching germs, for example, which leads to a dread of catching a terrible and possibly deadly illness. Most people are aware of germs and generally avoid them when they can, but a person obsessed with germs can think of little besides avoiding them. The person develops compulsive behaviors such as washing his or her hands over and over and may avoid all public places, even

When a person develops a pattern of compulsive behavior (such as excessively washing hands) to avoid an obsessive thought or worry, and when this behavior has a negative effect on living normally, the person is said to have an obsessive-compulsive disorder.

for necessary chores like grocery shopping. When a person develops a pattern of compulsive behavior to avoid an obsessive thought or worry, and when this behavior has a negative effect on living normally, the person is said to have an obsessive-compulsive disorder, or OCD.

According to the National Institute of Mental Health, OCD affects about 2.2 million adults in America and perhaps as many as 1 million children or teenagers. It involves rituals, sometimes bizarre ones, that people develop to avoid negative consequences such as getting sick or injured or having bad luck. Their behaviors may become like superstitions. They may engage in checking behavior, such as ensuring that their front door is locked by unlocking and locking it again, often many times, whenever they leave their home or apartment. Compulsive behaviors often turn into rituals. A person might feel compelled to turn a light switch on and off exactly fourteen times before leaving home, for example, and if the ritual is interrupted, he or she may feel the need to start all over to avoid bad consequences. Such behaviors can be time-consuming, weird, and embarrassing. About 80 percent of people with OCD are aware that their obsessions are not rational and their compulsive behaviors for

Hoarding, East and West

Hoarding has no known link to any particular racial or ethnic groups in the United States, but American society as a whole might be a breeding ground for hoarding behavior. In the United States, there is an endless supply of merchandise in any price range that can be readily bought or collected. Some researchers have questioned whether a widespread American fascination with material belongings may feed hoarders' compulsion to collect and keep far more stuff than they need. Studies carried out in other economically developed countries such as Japan, however, have found compulsive hoarding behavior there, too. Perhaps any society whose citizens can afford material things may create a cultural environment that enables or encourages hoarding. In any country, though, the factors that drive hoarding behavior seem to have more to do with genetics, coping mechanisms, traumatic experiences, and difficulty with organization than with greed or materialism. And while there are places in the world where hoarding is not an issue, this may be due to a lack of access to things one might hoard, rather than a cultural immunity to the behavior. The urge to collect and keep things may not be a cultural phenomenon, but simply a human one.

responding to these obsessive worries are not normal, yet they cannot bring themselves to stop.

MORE THAN JUST A DIRTY HOUSE

"There's so many facets to a problem like that. You don't want to just address the cleaning and not the other unmet needs in the person's life."—Miriam Callahan, information and assistance unit, Erie County Senior Services, New York

Quoted in Stephen T. Watson. "Shedding Light on Dirty Secret." *Buffalo (NY) News*, May 9, 2011. www.buffalonews.com/city/article417474.ece.

Hoarding has long been considered a type of OCD behavior, because people who hoard often worry obsessively about the emotional regret they might feel if they lose or throw away their possessions. They also develop a special behavior to cope with their dread—they keep and store everything that crosses their threshold. "The obsession that most often drives hoarding behavior is the thought that if a particular item is thrown away it will be gone forever and that someday the person may need it or something connected to it," says Cheryl Carmin, an expert in the treatment of hoarding and other anxiety disorders. "Rather than 'risk' not having the item when it's needed, the person saves it."[15] Some people who hoard also have superstitions about their belongings. They may believe that throwing items away will somehow cause something bad to happen to them or to people they care about. "[Some] people with hoarding behaviors have magical ideas about discarding material," says clinical psychologist Edna B. Foa. "For example, a person might not want to discard fingernail clippings or hair for fear that this would cause some harm to occur."[16] People who engage in hoarding behavior for reasons like these share many characteristics with people who have OCD.

Hoarding May Not Be an Obsession

On the other hand, hoarding does not always fit neatly into the OCD classification. The vast majority of people who hoard (about eight in ten) have no other OCD-like behaviors. Most hoarders do not, for instance, engage in rituals like checking door locks or repeatedly washing their hands. Also, whereas the majority of people with OCD realize their behavior is irrational and is negatively affecting their lives, hoarders far less commonly see their behavior as odd or troublesome. "An important difference between hoarding and OCD is evident in the extent to which the symptoms provoke discomfort and are viewed as repugnant," say social workers and hoarding experts Christiana Bratiotis, Cristina Sorrentino Schmalisch, and Gail Steketee. "People who hoard appear just as likely to embrace their behaviors ('my stuff is important; I need it') as to find them problematic. People with OCD usually recognize that their obsessions and compulsions are unreasonable and impairing."[17] This difference, to many experts, means hoarding may not quite fit with other OCDs.

Another reason that some psychologists do not consider hoarding as being part of OCD is that hoarding behavior usually has *two* parts. Most hoarders avoid throwing anything away in order to ward off sadness or perceived bad luck, but hoarding is not entirely about avoiding something unpleasant. Another important aspect of hoarding is acquiring new things and bringing them into one's home. This behavior, and often, merely being surrounded by one's many belongings, gives comfort and pleasure to a person who hoards. Therefore, hoarding is often as much about finding happiness or contentment in life as avoiding sadness or disaster. In this way hoarding may be more like an addiction than an OCD.

Addicted to "Stuff"

Unlike compulsions, which are behaviors developed to avoid something the person dreads, addictions are behaviors developed to seek something the person enjoys. Most people think of drugs, alcohol, and tobacco products when they hear the word *addiction*, because a person may become so dependent on the pleasurable feelings these substances provide that he or she might do almost anything to obtain them. Not all addictions involve the use of chemical substances, however. Many addictive behaviors develop simply because people feel happy or good about themselves when they do certain things, or because they hope that if they take part

Many hoarders share characteristics with compulsive gamblers.

in something, it will have a positive outcome. These ideas begin to control their thoughts and behavior.

Gambling is one activity that can grow into an addiction for people. Compulsive gamblers become obsessed with the idea that they could eventually become rich if they bet the right amount of money on the right thing. They dwell on the possibility of this positive outcome and take every possible opportunity to gamble. They are obsessed with never missing a chance to become wealthy, even though this behavior instead often leads to financial ruin. Many hoarders share characteristics with compulsive gamblers. They become obsessed with the possibility of opportunities. They constantly purchase, collect, or otherwise acquire new things because they believe those items might be useful in the future, and they think they might someday regret not buying or accepting the items when they had a chance. In this way acquiring, like gambling, becomes an addiction. "When people who compulsively buy or pick up free things 'lock on' to an item they want to obtain, they can't stop thinking about it," say Frost, Steketee, and hoarding expert David F. Tolin. "Their attention is so narrowly focused on the object and all the opportunities it could provide that they can't see what it will cost them in money, space, or trouble—until they get home."[18]

For whatever reasons they like to shop for new things, hoarders tend to purchase and bring home items they have no room to store. Often their new purchases, even those intended as gifts for other people, get lost in piles of items they already have. Still, hoarders continue acquiring even more things because they enjoy shopping and do not want to miss out on great sales or chances to get free stuff. Eventually, hoarders fill their living spaces with material acquired over many months or years. If a hoarder also becomes emotionally attached to objects or fears throwing out something that will later be important, the combination of addictively acquiring and compulsively keeping things can overrun the person's home and life.

Hoarding: In a Class of Its Own

Psychologists have learned that hoarding behavior is far more than being an unusually nostalgic person or than being untidy

Community Contributions

Animal hoarding is unique among hoarding behaviors in that the greater community often has an active role in creating the problem. Most communities have animal shelters filled beyond capacity with pets that need homes. Animals not adopted within a certain time frame may be euthanized. To encourage more people to adopt, shelters often advertise their pet populations with television commercials and news stories featuring homeless pets in a state of dire need. Those who hoard animals often start out as rescuers of such creatures, taking in pets that would likely be euthanized otherwise. They are often praised for doing the shelter, the animals, and the community a kind service. Neighbors and acquaintances may even bring unwanted pets to the neighborhood "pet collector" instead of abandoning the animals at a shelter. Over time, because of their unwillingness to turn a homeless creature away, people may acquire far too many animals to care for properly—sometimes hundreds of them. The animals may starve or get sick, leading the community to then accuse the person of hoarding and cruelty. However, the overabundance of other people's abandoned and neglected animals often contributes to pet hoarding in the first place.

Those who hoard animals often start out as rescuers. They take pets that would otherwise be euthanized from shelters, like the cat shelter pictured.

and procrastinating on housework. It is also more complex than being a shopaholic or an avid collector of things. These habits all contribute to hoarding, but the behavior is complicated and often very difficult to define because each case of hoarding is unique. Some hoarders are especially compulsive about saving things that could be useful someday. Other hoarders are primarily driven by the positive feelings they get from shopping or collecting. Still other hoarders mostly wish to avoid regret, sorrow, or bad karma that could result from throwing away things to which they have become attached. Most cases of hoarding represent some combination of all these factors.

Many psychologists who study hoarding and its causes, therefore, argue that hoarding behavior is neither addiction nor a branch of OCD, but its own unique behavior. "Within the psychiatric community, discussions are ongoing at the present time to determine whether hoarding should be classified as a separate mental health disorder (tentatively titled Hoarding Disorder),"[19] say Bratiotis, Schmalisch, and Steketee. The way hoarding is classified in psychology books and manuals is important because it helps doctors, counselors, and other mental health professionals understand what kinds of thoughts and feelings might drive a person to hoard in the first place. However, a diagnosis of hoarding is never one-size-fits-all. For mental health professionals interested in helping a person overcome hoarding, it is more important to understand the individual's personality and feelings than merely to diagnose his or her condition as a general type of disorder outlined in a psychology book or manual.

WHY PEOPLE HOARD

Hoarding has components of OCDs and addictive behaviors outlined in psychology manuals, but it also has ties to many other aspects of a person's life. Hoarding is a complicated and usually lifelong behavior. It often is connected to complex emotions, memories, and fears. Hoarding may be linked to insecurity and to personality traits as well. The behavior has even been associated with certain abnormalities in the way people's brains function. The more psychologists study hoarding and the people who do it, the more they realize that hoarding is usually the result of at least one and often several underlying causes. To treat the condition, doctors and scientists must first understand and deal with its origins, and these may be very different from one hoarder to the next.

An Early Start to Hoarding

Although the causes of hoarding vary widely, hoarding behavior usually begins at a young age. The first signs of hoarding are often present in children and teenagers. However, identifying someone as a hoarder so early in life is difficult for a number of reasons. First, many young people are naturally messy and reluctant to clean their rooms without being nagged about it by their parents or guardians. This is not necessarily a sign of a future hoarding problem, and people who do hoard later in life may not have realized they were doing anything different than a lot of other kids when they were young. Another thing that makes early hoarding hard to differentiate from normal childhood behavior is that most children tend to form emotional attachments to certain things, such as special stuffed animals, that

Although hoarding usually starts at an early age, many young people are naturally messy and reluctant to clean their rooms without being nagged about it by their parents or guardians. This is not necessarily a sign of a future hoarding problem.

they would feel heartbroken to throw out or give away. Being overly attached to objects can be a sign of future hoarding tendencies for some people, but most children eventually outgrow their intense attachment to things like their toys and develop a more realistic sense of what should have sentimental value. It is often difficult to tell whether attachment to objects is a sign of future hoarding or just a common trait that the child will outgrow in time.

A third thing that makes it difficult to identify early signs of hoarding behavior is that most children are natural collectors of

pretty or interesting items. Toy manufacturers capitalize on this fact all the time, producing certain toys in many different styles or colors and then urging kids to collect the whole set. Acquiring strange things or many more of a particular item than one actually needs is not uncommon behavior for kids, so it is hard to identify future hoarders based on this trait alone. Because children and teens live at home with other family members who may

Children form attachments to certain toys or stuffed animals and like collecting them, which does not necessarily lead to hoarding as an adult.

clean up after them or help them to clean and organize their own living spaces regularly, their early signs of hoarding behavior may be unnoticeable at a young age or may not stand out as different from what most other kids the same age are doing. It often takes many years of living on their own for hoarders to accumulate so much stuff that they are no longer comfortable in their environment. Family members and friends of kids who have early signs of hoarding, therefore, may just think they know an untidy child or one who likes to collect things. These are not necessarily signs of hoarding. "There are so many kids who never achieve order, and they're still normal," says Eric Storch, a psychologist who studies hoarding behavior. "A messy room isn't hoarding, it's just a messy room."[20]

HELPING THE HELPLESS

"I think the hoarding word is used too much. . . . The issue is not hoarding. I'm just concerned with a helpless animal that doesn't have a voice and nobody cares. I feel harassed when people are trying to make a problem for me."—Loyce Ogden, found guilty in 2008 of animal cruelty charges after one hundred dead cats were removed from her Springfield, Ohio, home

Quoted in Katie Wedell and Mark McGregor. "Taxpayers Often Bear Costs to Clean Up After Hoarders." *Springfield (OH) News-Sun*, October 3, 2011. www.springfieldnews sun.com/news/springfield-news/taxpayers-often-bear-costs-to-clean-up-after-hoarders -1263492.html.

Nevertheless, many adults who have a problem with hoarding say their behavior began when they were young. Looking back, they can often identify a certain trigger from their early life, a particular experience that started the hoarding behavior. Most hoarding behavior is associated with emotional trauma. Kids, teenagers, and even adults who live through a challenging situation may begin to hoard as a coping mechanism, a method of adjusting to or dealing with stress. "Most hoarders have psychological and social histories beginning in childhood that are chaotic and traumatic," say social services experts Arnold Arluke and Celeste Killeen. "The

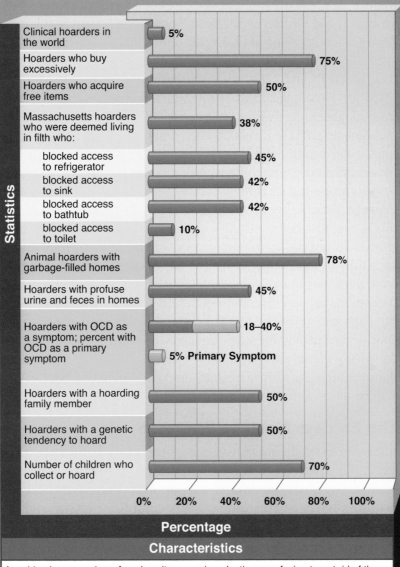

Hoarding Statistics and Characteristics

Statistics (vertical axis)

Statistic	Percentage
Clinical hoarders in the world	5%
Hoarders who buy excessively	75%
Hoarders who acquire free items	50%
Massachusetts hoarders who were deemed living in filth who:	38%
blocked access to refrigerator	45%
blocked access to sink	42%
blocked access to bathtub	42%
blocked access to toilet	10%
Animal hoarders with garbage-filled homes	78%
Hoarders with profuse urine and feces in homes	45%
Hoarders with OCD as a symptom; percent with OCD as a primary symptom	18–40% / 5% Primary Symptom
Hoarders with a hoarding family member	50%
Hoarders with a genetic tendency to hoard	50%
Number of children who collect or hoard	70%

Percentage (horizontal axis: 0% 20% 40% 60% 80% 100%)

Characteristics

Acquiring large number of useless items and neglecting or refusing to get rid of them.

Cluttering living spaces to the point they cannot be used for their intended purpose.

Being unable to return borrowed items, sometimes leading to theft.

Evolutionary, in that some speculate that hoarding was once advantageous and has been preserved in certain family lines.

Children begin collecting objects at 25 months of age.

Common personality traits of hoarders include neuroticism, anxiety, depression, self-conciousness, and indecisiveness.

Taken from: www.psychologydegree.net.

vast majority [of hoarders] report feelings of insecurity and disruptive experiences early in life, including frequent relocations, parental separation and divorce, and isolation from peers."[21] Even people who do not begin hoarding until they are adults usually can remember a specific event that was emotionally hard for them. In response to it they began to find comfort by surrounding themselves with belongings. "Hoarding affords many of its sufferers the illusion of control and replaces fear with a feeling of safety,"[22] say psychologists and hoarding researchers Randy O. Frost and Gail Steketee.

Mental health professionals once believed that hoarding behavior developed in people who had been very poor as children or were deprived of things like clothing, toys, and even food. However, studies on hoarding since the 1990s have shown that this is not always the case. Having few personal belongings as a child does not necessarily make a person more likely to hoard as an adult. In fact, many hoarders grew up in families that had enough money to live comfortably. What these young people did lack, perhaps, was love and emotional support from their families. "We knew that the common wisdom of hoarding being a response to deprivation was not the whole story," say Frost and Steketee. "Plenty of hoarders have lived comfortable lives. But deprivation is not always material, and emotional deprivation can also be devastating."[23]

The Endless Need to Stock Up

Although many hoarders can recognize a link between a traumatic event from their past and the time their hoarding behavior started, emotional trauma is not the only thing that leads to hoarding behavior. Hoarding is a very complicated issue, and for many people, it is also strongly linked to certain personality traits. Hoarders tend to be intelligent and creative, and some psychologists believe hoarders actually see the world differently than most nonhoarders do. They might be very detail oriented, for example, and take time to appreciate the beauty or usefulness of objects that most people ignore. Many hoarders are crafty or artistic and may develop a habit of collecting cloth scraps, beads, trinkets, paint, or other things they come across that they believe they might use to create something useful or pretty. Unfortunately, hoarders may collect to such a degree that they eventually feel overwhelmed by the sheer volume of their supplies. "People who hoard often come up with idea after idea, saving things for all kinds of creative reasons but never following through with those plans," say Frost, Steketee, and hoarding expert David F. Tolin. "They have become victims of their own creativity."[24]

Whereas some hoarders collect items for creative purposes, other hoarders are enthralled by information. They may keep vast stacks of newspapers, magazines, newsletters, brochures, and other published materials because these things are brimming with facts that the hoarder finds useful or interesting. Hoarders may believe that they will one day get around to reading every old newspaper and magazine in their home. Meanwhile, new information arrives every day, so hoarders quickly accumulate far more material than they will ever have time to process. The hoarder's ambition "exceeds his or her physical capacity to carry out the plans," say Tolin, Frost, and Steketee. "The brain writes checks that the body can't cash."[25]

Many hoarders are also driven by a constant need to feel prepared. Almost anything they come across may have a potential use or purpose, so some hoarders worry about tossing out things they might one day need and regret having thrown away. Hoarders tend to be perfectionists in that they often fear making mistakes they cannot fix, such as passing up an opportunity to purchase a unique item or throwing out something that later turns out to have been important. Hoarders often accumulate truly useful things, such as canned food, batteries, clothing, and blankets, but in amounts greater than they ever end up needing. They may also keep things such as stacks of paper napkins or salt and pepper packets from fast food restaurants, because they hate to waste things. Since hoarders can usually think of a possible purpose for almost anything in their home, nothing is really "junk" to them. They can usually make an argument for keeping all of their things—at least an argument that makes sense to *them*.

Faulty Memories

Another personality trait that troubles many hoarders is that they lack faith in their ability to recall things. Hoarders often fear that if they throw out souvenirs, photographs, or other mementos that symbolize important people and experiences in their lives, the people and experiences themselves might disappear from memory. "For some people, these items serve as a tangible record of their lives," say Tolin, Frost, and Steketee. "Throwing them away feels like losing that part of their lives."[26] Most college graduates, for example, might keep their degree in a frame on the wall as a way to mark the years they spent in school, but hoarders might keep every textbook, term paper, test, and notebook, fearing that if they throw these things out, the knowledge they gained will

While normal college graduates might keep their earned degree and frame it on the wall, hoarders might keep every textbook, term paper, test, and notebook, fearing that if they throw these things out, the knowledge they gained will disappear, too.

disappear, too. Few hoarders spend time going through such materials regularly, though. Instead, they put items in boxes or stacks and pile more and more stuff on top as years go by. Eventually they bury and possibly forget about the very items they were so anxious to remember.

Hoarders usually realize they tend to forget about things that are out of sight, but this does not lead to the conclusion that it is okay to throw those things away. Instead, it may only convince hoarders that their ability to process and hold onto memories is even worse than they believed. "The clients we have seen who engage in memory hoarding compulsions are concerned that moments in time will pass without them fully understanding, remembering, and appreciating them,"[27] says Jon Hershfield, a psychotherapist who often works with hoarders. Since many hoarders believe that information must be kept in plain sight until they have a chance to fully process it, the result is often a living space filled to the brim with written information. A particular bill might go on the top of a stack of other bills and papers, for example, to remind the hoarder to see it and pay it. Ironically, the bill is likely to get buried beneath other things that the hoarder feels are also important enough to be on the top of the stack and in plain sight. In this way "important" things are merely shuffled around in a hoarder's ever-growing piles, and information becomes even more likely to be forgotten. Hoarders then blame their faulty memory, not their poorly organized homes, and insist all the more strongly on the impossible task of keeping all their important things in sight at once.

The Disorganized Hoarder

Because hoarders so commonly feel the need to keep everything in plain view in order to remember it, psychologists have also studied the way hoarders think about and classify their thousands of mementos. Hoarders generally approach the process of organization far differently than people who do not hoard. Most people see their world in large categories and organize their surroundings and their belongings accordingly. Rooms of a typical house, for example, are already arranged for the activities people do at home—grooming in the bathroom, sleeping in the bedroom, cooking and eating in the kitchen, and relaxing in the family room. Things a family will need for cooking are then stored in the kitchen, hairstyling supplies are kept in the bathroom, and so on. For most people, finding a particular item can be accomplished fairly quickly by going to the area where that item is most likely to be used and therefore stored.

People who hoard do not seem to classify their belongings into such predictable categories. Instead, some psychologists believe hoarders organize in terms of empty space. When they see a vacant spot, they think that is the perfect place to put something important—they will be more likely to see it there and remember it. As they collect more and more things, they gradually fill up empty spaces in their homes—on the floor, under tables and chairs, on countertops, on top of other stacks. Many hoarders do not have logical organizing systems, nor do they always classify things with other similar things. When they buy new clothes, they might not put the clothes in the closet, or even in the bedroom, but may add them to the top of a stack of unrelated things in the kitchen or bathroom. Psychologists believe that hoarders tend to see each of their belongings as being in its own category. To find a particular pair of shoes, therefore, they do not first begin in the place where they keep all of their shoes. They instead expect themselves to remember where they put that one pair of shoes in the piles of other things.

For most hoarders, finding anything becomes very difficult and frustrating. They may even go out and buy a replacement for something they own because they think it will take too much time to find the one they already have. Many do not realize that they have difficulty categorizing items and information. Instead, they blame what they think is their faulty memory when they lose something. Adding to the problem is that many hoarders become easily distracted and may have symptoms of attention-deficit/hyperactivity disorder (ADHD), a mental disorder that makes it difficult to concentrate, complete tasks, organize information, and remember to perform certain daily activities. Hoarders who have symptoms of ADHD tend to be very easily distracted. Therefore, sitting down to sort through and categorize huge piles of belongings becomes difficult or even impossible. "For people with compulsive hoarding, the distractions are more frequent, more intense, and more compelling" than for people who do not have difficulty focusing their attention, say Tolin, Frost, and Steketee. Often, "the distractions come from inside, rather than outside, the person,"[28] because he or she spends so much time thinking of creative reasons to keep each item pulled out of the pile. Being easily distracted makes organizing and sorting a monumental task for hoarders, one they typically dread and avoid. A hoarder's living environment thus gets more cluttered and disorganized as the years go by.

Nature Versus Nurture

Scientists have long suspected that there is also a biological basis for hoarding behavior, because a large majority of people who hoard (80 percent or more) report having a first-degree relative—a parent or a sibling—who also hoards. Genetic studies of families with multiple hoarders have shown that there is a particular gene that tends to be present in hoarders but not in nonhoarders. Hoarding behavior, therefore, might actually be genetic and inherited. Many psychologists, however, argue that hoarders who grew up in a household of another hoarder may simply have learned the behavior from parents or siblings. After watching piles of clutter grow and never being taught how to organize, sort through, and prioritize their own belongings, hoarders might only be doing what they learned as children to do—save everything, waste nothing, and pile stuff on every clear surface of their home.

Calling hoarding a genetic disorder may make hoarders feel less responsible for their situation and reduce feelings of self-blame. However, it can also create hopelessness for hoarders if it leads them to believe the behavior is inevitable. Calling hoarding a learned behavior, on the other hand, may be helpful because it gives hoarders hope that they can "unlearn" their bad habits and get better about organizing their belongings and ridding their homes of clutter. This can backfire, however, if hoarders struggle to "unlearn" their behavior and start blaming themselves for what may actually be a genetic inability to easily correct the problem. Many psychologists believe hoarding stems from a combination of both genetics and learned behaviors. "For a condition like compulsive hoarding to come about, you probably have to have a person who has a certain set of inherited characteristics," says Tolin, but "that person then has to in some way *learn* or *pick up* the behavioral pattern. . . . Biology is not destiny."[29]

Safekeepers

Whether hoarding is genetic or not, brain studies on hoarders have shown that many might have at least one other thing in common. A brain-picturing process called functional magnetic resonance imaging (fMRI) can be used to examine activity in various parts of the brain that are associated with emotional thoughts and activities. When people who took part in one hoarding study were asked to think about discarding possessions while their brains were being examined by fMRI, certain emotion-related areas of the brain became more active in the hoarders than in the people who did not hoard. These results suggested that there may be a physical difference in brain structure and function that gives hoarders an intense emotional attachment to their belongings.

A DRAWN-OUT DEATH

"[People who hoard animals] have no real perception of the harm they're doing to the animals. Being kept by a hoarder is a slow kind of death for the animal. Actually, it can be a fate worse than death."—Randall Lockwood, senior vice president of forensic sciences and anti-cruelty projects, American Society for the Prevention of Cruelty to Animals (ASPCA)

Quoted in American Society for the Prevention of Cruelty to Animals. "Animal Hoarding." www.aspca.org/fight-animal-cruelty/animal-hoarding.aspx.

Indeed, many hoarders *do* feel a strong connection to things that most other people would not find important. What might look like junk to an observer can be a treasure trove of personally important items for the hoarder. Even though most hoarders, by definition, live among disorganized piles of stuff that has limited value, they tend to feel uneasy if someone moves or even touches any of their things. Many hoarders are extremely protective of their belongings. Some even see themselves as "safekeepers," giving a safe refuge to objects that need it.

Hoarders may even imagine human characteristics in their belongings. This phenomenon is called anthropomorphizing, from the root words *anthropos* (human) and *morph* (to change or transform). Hoarders may believe some of their things have actual personalities and feelings. Even nonhoarders anthropomorphize from time to time. Some people give a name and an imagined personality to their automobile, for example. Others become emotionally attached to things like a favorite armchair that they begin to think has its own personality. Anthropomorphizing an object makes it seem more personal, unique, and important. For people who imagine that objects have human-like qualities, it becomes much more

Many hoarders, like Becky Barton (pictured), feel a strong connection to things other people would find unimportant.

difficult to throw things out or give them away. Hoarders may engage in this behavior to a greater extent than most other people. "Their anthropomorphizing of objects is intense," Frost says, and it often begins at an early age. "One kid we saw spilled Kool-Aid on the sidewalk and was upset because the Kool-Aid was being hurt,"[30] Frost recalls. Hoarders who anthropomorphize may live among piles of items that, to them, have true personalities, and they might feel a strong need to love and care for their things.

This safekeeping behavior is nowhere more pronounced than in people who hoard animals. Pets are far different than inanimate objects in that they actually do have personalities of their own. People who keep pets often feel the animals are members of the family and may grieve profoundly when a pet dies. People with hoarding tendencies can take these normal feelings about pets to

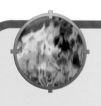

Inside the World of Animal Hoarding

Animal hoarding is a particularly burdensome type of hoarding behavior. Unlike inanimate objects, animals bear direct costs and responsibilities that cannot be ignored. At a minimum they require food and water, shelter, opportunities and space to exercise and play, and veterinary care if they become sick. Hoarders may keep dozens or even hundreds of animals in their homes, creating a huge financial burden in the cost of food and care and often rendering them unable to provide adequately for their pets' other needs. Animals in these situations are almost always underfed, sick with respiratory and other illnesses, and poorly groomed or cared for. The hoarders themselves may suffer as well. Their homes are often filled with animal waste to the point of rotten floorboards and indoor air concentrations of ammonia (a chemical given off in animal urine) greatly in excess of what people can safely breathe. Animal hoarding has the unique potential to create squalor and illness, yet hoarders usually deny that their home or animals are in poor condition. And because many animal hoarders feel that their animals are their family, convincing them to part with even some of their companions can be a long, painful, and trying process.

extremes, seeing every animal they encounter as an individual friend and often seeing themselves as caretakers and safekeepers of animals in need. Hoarders who place themselves into this role usually feel a strong sense of responsibility to animals. They may acquire new ones wherever they go, taking in stray cats and dogs, adopting from animal shelters and pet stores, and always looking for another critter who needs a loving home.

Animal hoarders tend to share other hoarders' impulsive behavior and inability to make good decisions about how many things they can logically bring home and find a place for. They may also become addicted to finding new animals because of the good feelings they get from rescuing a homeless creature. Many animal hoarders see themselves as the only ones who could care for their pets properly. The idea of parting with even one of a usually large assortment of animals can create intense feelings of anguish. "Animal hoarders often believe they have a special gift for empathizing with animals, and that care for animals is their life's mission," says veterinarian and animal protection activist Gary Patronek. "With this in mind, it is easy to appreciate the intense feelings of loss when an animal must be given up."[31]

FIRST, DO NO HARM

"When you go into a home and see animals all sickly and crawling with parasites, that's pretty heart-wrenching. But it's important to note that these people don't see themselves as doing anything wrong—a lot of the time they think they're saving the animals."—Lynn Reid, animal control officer, Fairfax County, Virginia

Quoted in Leah Fabel. "Local Task Forces Target Dangerous Hoarding." *Washington (DC) Examiner,* July 13, 2011. http://washingtonexaminer.com/local/virginia/2011/07/area-task -forces-target-dangerous-hoarding#ixzz1fGW7wz5l.

Unfortunately, animal hoarders may have even greater attachment to their belongings than those who hoard objects, and they are also the ones whose hoarding behavior is most likely to develop serious consequences. Cramming numerous animals into one's home or yard can rapidly create an unclean and unsafe

Digital Uncluttering

Reading materials are among the most commonly hoarded items. What may start out as a few saved books or newspapers can grow into a towering problem after a few years. Few people think of books and papers as dangerous items, but when saved by the hundreds or thousands, they can be. If a heavy stack of books were to fall on somebody, it could cause serious injury. Paper reading materials also provide fuel for a raging blaze if a hoarder's home catches fire.

Modern technology may be able to help eliminate these hoarded hazards from people's homes. E-readers like the Kindle and the Nook can store thousands of books, newspapers, and magazines in the amount of space occupied by a single paperback. They make it easy, private, and practical for people to keep all the information they want without visibly storing it in their living spaces. Unfortunately, hoarders may resist using e-readers for precisely this reason. Most like to have all their belongings out and visible. They may reject the idea of digital storage, genuinely preferring to keep their books and newspapers in bulky physical form. This renders e-readers useless for many hoarders.

Modern technology like the Kindle can help eliminate the hazardous hoarded paper reading material from people's homes.

environment, both for the animals and for the people who share the home. Animal hoarders' intentions are often good—they usually believe they are caring for animals that would otherwise be homeless and might die. However, the inability to make realistic decisions about how many pets they should acquire and what to do when they have too many animals means the situation, for many hoarders, soon escalates to a disaster. Hoarding of animals has many of the same causes as hoarding of objects, but when a person hoards animals that make noise and produce large volumes of waste, it becomes much harder to hide hoarding behavior from the outside world. Animal hoarders, even more than people who hoard nonliving objects, have brought about a great deal of societal awareness in recent years about the often serious and wide-reaching effects of hoarding behavior, both on hoarders themselves and those around them.

The Hidden Costs of Hoarding

Hoarding behavior develops for many different reasons, but whatever causes it, hoarding does not become a problem overnight. It may take years, even decades, for enough collected stuff to overwhelm a person's living space and begin to have a truly negative effect on his or her life. Because hoarding is a problem that worsens gradually, many hoarders see themselves as cluttered or messy but not necessarily as having a mental disorder. Years of being used to a cluttered home may blind some hoarders to the fact that their situation is getting slowly but steadily worse. "Those who hoard are less likely to have insight" into their problem, say social workers and hoarding experts Christiana Bratiotis, Cristina Sorrentino Schmalisch, and Gail Steketee, "for example, saying 'I like it this way' and 'I'm not causing anyone any harm.'"[32] Unfortunately, hoarding often does cause a lot of people considerable harm, even if the hoarders themselves cannot see it or will not admit it. Hoarding has serious consequences and can cost people in terms of money, health, personal relationships, and even legal freedom.

The Cost of Acquiring and Storing

One negative effect of hoarding is that it can be a costly habit. Some hoarders are shopaholics, people who actively seek out the good feelings they get from buying new things. They may have a tendency to act impetuously—they focus completely on their immediate want or need to own a new thing. Only later, after spending the money, do they think about whether they could really afford the item, whether they needed it, or whether they have a place to store it.

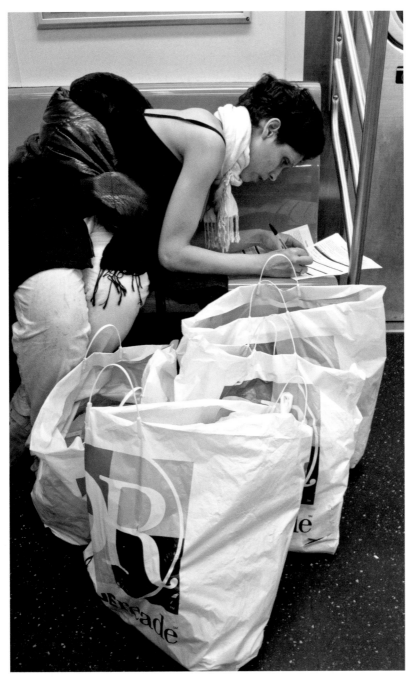

Some hoarders are "shopaholics," people who actively seek out the good feelings they get from buying new things.

Constantly acquiring new items can be a very expensive pastime. Hoarders who like to shop for new things might use credit cards to make their purchases. If they do not pay their full credit card balance each month, the credit company charges interest. A percentage of whatever portion of the balance remains unpaid then gets added to the bill for the following month, and thus, the amount owed grows steadily over time. Hoarders who buy impulsively, using credit cards without thinking of whether they can afford the items they are buying, can quickly amass credit card debt on which they must also pay interest. Furthermore, hoarders may eventually spend the maximum amount their credit cards allow, so if they have an emergency and need money for something like a health problem or a home or vehicle repair, they will not be able to use credit cards for that purpose. Irresponsible buying is one way hoarding can cost a person financially.

Of course, not all hoarders overspend to buy new things. Many can either afford their buying habits or prefer to collect things that are low-cost or free. They may accumulate large piles of brochures and pamphlets, for example, or items from second-hand stores or free samples of things. Some hoarders even collect items they spy in other people's trash, thinking certain objects are useful or pretty and should not go to waste. Even when hoarders are not overspending to acquire new items, however, their behavior can still cause financial troubles. "Once people who hoard bring something into their homes," say psychologists Michael A. Tompkins and Tamara L. Hartl, "it becomes almost impossible to get it out again."[33] Living spaces begin to fill up with stuff, and a hoarder must find somewhere to put it all. Hoarders often try to solve the problem by purchasing storage sheds for their yard or renting storage units, garage-sized spaces usually leased for a monthly or yearly fee. If the compulsive acquiring and saving behaviors do not stop, however, adding storage is just a temporary fix. "Storage spaces are meant to free up living space, but soon, both spaces are full,"[34] say hoarding researchers Fugen Neziroglu, Jill Slaven, and Katharine Donnelly. Hoarders must then spend money on even more storage space or live among ever-growing piles of clutter.

An Increased Cost of Living

A third way hoarding can create financial burden is in the cost of food. Hoarders' kitchens are often so cluttered that they cannot prepare or cook meals on countertops or the stove. Cupboards, refrigerators, and ovens may be used to store objects instead of groceries. "Families are often unable to use their kitchens to cook food and may, therefore, be dependent on ordering takeout daily," say Neziroglu, Slaven, and Donnelly. "This may lead to financial strain and obesity, because they are spending more money and taking in more calories than they would if they were able to make their own meals."[35] For those who hoard animals, food is a more pressing problem still. Pet food is expensive, and the cost of feeding dozens of dogs, cats, birds, or other critters every day can quickly overwhelm a person financially. Some who hoard animals spend more money feeding their pets than feeding themselves, so the quality of their own nutrition may suffer as much as their pocketbooks.

Adding even more to the financial strain of hoarding is that it often takes many years for clutter to reach problematic proportions. By the time hoarding gets bad enough to start costing a lot of money, hoarders may have retired from their jobs. Many hoarders are elderly and live on fixed incomes—a limited amount of money received each month from retirement funds. If they are spending this money on new items, storage space for the things they already own, takeout meals, and/or food for their pets, hoarders may find they are unable to afford other things they want or need, such as health care or utilities like power and heat.

For hoarders who own their own homes, an additional problem is that homeowners' insurance rates may escalate if the insurance company discovers that the person hoards. Hoarding behavior can create household dangers that make it more likely for a fire or other home disaster to occur, so some insurance companies charge more to insure the home of a hoarder. To avoid stiff insurance premiums, hoarders might feel forced to become even more secretive about their behavior or may choose not to insure their home at all, which means that following a disaster such as a house fire, they would not receive any insurance reimbursements and could lose all that they own.

Unwelcome Inhabitants

A hoarding lifestyle not only costs money, it can also cost hoarders their own well-being. The home of someone with a severe hoarding problem can be a dangerous, unhealthy place to live. Neziroglu, Slaven, and Donnelly go so far as to say, "For those family members who live with a person who hoards, it is impossible to live in the clutter and not have physical and emotional trauma."[36] Hoarding that has gone on for many years usually results in a home whose rooms are overflowing with piles of items. It is very difficult to effectively clean living spaces so cluttered that paths must be formed just to get from one room to the next. "As clutter develops and stays, it becomes impossible to remove accumulated dust from spaces that are most affected because people are not able to vacuum or dust their homes, sometimes for years,"[37] say Neziroglu, Slaven, and Donnelly. Dirt and dust can eventually cause breathing problems for a home's inhabitants, who may develop allergies or asthma due to constantly breathing in dust particles floating in the air.

Another unsanitary problem in many hoarding homes is that hoarders may hesitate to throw out almost anything, even perishable items like food. If fruit, vegetables, meat, and dairy products are not properly disposed of, they begin to decompose, leading to bad smells and the presence of bacteria that can make the home's inhabitants sick. Rotting food can also attract pests into the home, and this is another significant problem for many hoarders. If insects like cockroaches invade the home and steps are not taken to remove them, their population eventually grows so large that swarms of them may be present in the clutter of every room. "A colleague of ours who is an expert on hoarding once described visiting a hoarder whose apartment walls were literally covered by cockroaches, to the point where it took him a moment to realize what was causing the walls to look like they were moving,"[38] says hoarding therapist Cheryl Carmin. Cockroaches shed tiny particles of their bodies into the air, causing allergies and breathing problems for the estimated one in five people (especially children) who are allergic to them. Cockroaches can also spread around harmful bacteria like E. coli and salmonella, putting a home's inhabitants at risk of food-borne illness.

Some hoarders may hesitate to throw out perishable food items. If fruit, vegetables, meat, and dairy products are not properly disposed of, they begin to decompose, leading to bad smells and the presence of bacteria that can make the home's inhabitants sick.

Rodents like rats and mice might also infest a hoarder's home, feasting on food items that were never thrown out and building nests in the piles of clutter. Rodents have large litters of offspring, so once they move into a hoarder's cluttered home and begin to breed, the problem usually gets much worse very quickly. "Mice and rats, when they are present, contribute most unpleasantly to dust," says Cheryl Mendelson, an author and researcher who studies the risks of not adequately cleaning one's living spaces. "Besides leaving hair and dander, as all furry creatures do, mice dribble urine as they explore in order to mark where they have been. They also drop feces a dozen times a day, and these droppings carry allergens and sometimes disease."[39] Rodents living in piles of clutter in one's home can be unnerving, and they pose a significant source of potential illness for the home's inhabitants.

Problems with Pets

People who hoard animals may have even greater sanitary problems in their homes than people who only hoard items. Furry pets like dogs and cats are constantly shedding hair and dander, or flakes of skin. When there are many of these animals in a person's home, the hair and dander alone can create dust and worsen air quality over time. This leads to problems such as allergies and asthma, conditions that can cause discomfort and sometimes a serious struggle to breathe due to swollen nasal passages and airways. Chronic wheezing and difficulty catching one's breath are common complications for animal hoarders and any family members who live with them.

The most immediate danger for pet hoarders, however, is usually feces and urine, which animals produce in great amounts. The more animals one owns, the more animal waste will begin to accumulate. Hoarders may own dozens to hundreds of animals, making it difficult or impossible to clean up all the urine and feces the animals produce. Homes of animal hoarders are often very unhygienic. "Floors may buckle from being soaked with urine and feces," say social services experts Arnold Arluke and Celeste Killeen. "Sanitary conditions frequently deteriorate to the point where dwellings are unfit for human habitation."[40] The air in the home of an animal hoarder may have dangerous levels of ammonia,

Crimes Against Canines

In January 2003, on the outskirts of the small town of Harper, Oregon, police went to the rented home of Barbara and Robert Erickson to follow up on complaints from neighbors that there were multiple dogs caged or kenneled outside the small house without adequate shelter from the rain and the muddy ground. Deputies found about 200 dogs living outdoors without adequate shelter. When they entered the residence, they found it overcrowded with animals as well. Investigators counted 552 dogs on the premises, 300 of them living inside the small, two-bedroom home. There were no clean areas for the dogs to sleep. Many had upper respiratory infections and mange, a skin disease caused by tiny parasites called mites. Most were underweight and undernourished. Investigators believe that some of the dogs even fought over limited food sources and may have killed weaker dogs and newborn puppies to eat them. The Ericksons were arrested on 552 misdemeanor charges of animal neglect and abuse and a felony charge of criminal mischief because their animal hoarding did irreparable damage to the home they were renting. They were sentenced to sixty months of probation and fined fifteen thousand dollars. The case was one of the largest seizures of hoarded animals in U.S. history.

a chemical produced in urine and whose fumes can be poisonous, even fatal, if breathed in large amounts. Feces also carry bacteria that can make people and animals sick, so when they are left on the floor and the furniture of a home, they pose a serious health risk to inhabitants. People who own many birds can also get respiratory illnesses such as aspergillosis, which comes from breathing in spores of a fungus that grows in accumulated piles of bird droppings. Many animal hoarders, along with their animal companions, suffer severe health complications due to living alongside the waste produced by so many critters.

Firetraps and Other Hazards

Homes of hoarders are dangerous to live in for other reasons beyond being unsanitary. For one thing, hoarding creates an environment in which house fires are more likely to start. The leading causes of house fires are related to cooking, heating, and electricity. A kitchen stove surrounded by stacks of paper or other

Unfortunately, severe hoarding behavior often leads to homes that are almost impossible to navigate, like the one pictured in which an elderly couple was found buried alive.

flammable clutter creates a dangerous situation, as does a radiator or heater vent piled with stuff, or a frayed electrical cord that is buried beneath cloth or paper. Clutter, which for many hoarders consists largely of things like newspapers and cardboard boxes, also creates ample fuel for flames to engulf a hoarder's home quickly if a fire does get started.

Unfortunately, severe hoarding behavior often leads to homes that are almost impossible to navigate except using the paths the hoarder has created. Windows may be blocked by piles of clutter. There may be clear access to only one door in the home, so in the event of a house fire, inhabitants may have very few escape routes. A burning building can quickly fill with smoke, disorienting the people inside and making it hard or impossible to find what may be the only way out of an overly cluttered home. The odds of dying in a house fire are significantly higher for someone who lives in heavy clutter, and also for anyone who enters the burning home to attempt a rescue. "It has escalated to the point where hoarding is injuring our firefighters,"[41] says Mike Reichling, public information officer for the Tempe, Arizona, Fire Department.

A hoarder's habits can also create a danger of collapse. In some hoarding cases piles of stored items have toppled over and buried people beneath hundreds of pounds of material. Hoarders can also create a situation where their entire home becomes structurally unstable. A home's attic, for example, is a common place for hoarders to move piles of things for storage, but most attics are not designed or built to support what might amount to tons of material moved there over the years. Hoarders' attics have been known to give out or collapse beneath the weight of hoarded piles of things, and this could crush people in the rooms below. This is yet another way hoarding often results in unhealthy and unsafe living spaces, not just for hoarders but for anyone who lives with them or enters their home.

The Social Consequences of Hoarding

Because of the often dangerous living environment hoarders may create, their behavior can have negative effects on their happiness and lifestyle as well as their safety. Isolation is one of the worst consequences. Even if hoarders feel comfortable living among dozens of pets or within their own towering piles of belongings, they are usually aware that their lifestyle is different than most people's and that others may be uncomfortable coming over to visit. "Hoarders often feel socially isolated, too embarrassed to let others see how they live,"[42] says Beth Ann McNeill, an emergency medical responder who has worked with hoarding patients. Hoarders may hesitate to invite friends or family members over, and even if they do extend an invitation, the friends or family members may turn it down because they are uncomfortable in the hoarder's home. "Living alone or isolated can lead to loneliness, depression, reduction in self care, increased risk of falls, and the inability to see health problems in oneself,"[43] says McNeill. Because hoarding is a long-term, often even lifelong problem, hoarders tend to suffer more and more from these effects of isolation as years go by.

Hoarding behavior may also strain the relationships of hoarders who are married or living with a significant other. Hoarding can cause many arguments. Often, the state of the hoarder's living environment, his or her refusal to let others sort through belongings, and illogical decisions about buying new things become overwhelming for living companions. If the hoarder does not agree to get help for the problem or is not emotionally ready to clean out the hoarded items or get rid of pets, an important human relationship in the person's life might end in a breakup or a divorce. Unfortunately, hoarding behavior is often already linked to traumatic events in a person's life and may be a coping mechanism for dealing with emotional problems. Therefore, when an important relationship in the person's life ends, even if this is a direct consequence of hoarding, the hoarder may respond to the new trauma by hoarding more as a way to cope. Feeling abandoned, the hoarder often becomes even more isolated, sad, and alone.

Hoarding's Collateral Damage

Hoarding behavior can impact the emotional well-being not just of the person who hoards but of anyone who lives in the home. A hoarder's living companions may be the ones who suffer most from the negative consequences of hoarding. Adult companions can and often do choose to leave a hoarder's home, but children of hoarders may feel completely powerless over their parents' hoarding behavior and also powerless to leave. Hoarding parents, ashamed of the condition of the home, may forbid children to have guests. Ashamed of their living environment, children of hoarders often voluntarily isolate themselves from their peers as well, sometimes going to great lengths to avoid having their peers see the inside of their home or even know where they live. "Nobody understands the weirdness of growing up this way unless they go through it,"[44] says Tracy Schroeder, the now-grown daughter of a hoarder. Many kids of hoarders grow up feeling lonely and may resent their parents for it, often claiming that their mom or dad cares more about "stuff" than about his or her own children.

Hoarding's effects may persist even when children of hoarders grow up and leave home. Statistics show that children of hoarders are at risk of becoming hoarders themselves, perhaps because they learned the behavior from their parents or because they are trying to cope with their own emotionally traumatic history. On the other hand, grown children of hoarders might fear the hoarding lifestyle and become overly concerned about clutter. As a result, they may buy and keep almost nothing. They may never want to go back to their parents' home. They might have children of their own but be embarrassed or ashamed to let their kids visit a hoarding grandparent. Hoarders, meanwhile, may feel as if their grown children do not love them because they never come to visit. In this way, even though hoarders may think their lifestyle is no one's business but theirs, hoarding is not always a private problem. It can have serious effects on a person and on a family for generations. In fact, hoarding can even have legal consequences regarding children, families, and property.

Hoarding and the Law

One important legal issue that surrounds hoarding stems from divorce. Whenever two spouses decide to end a marriage, they also must decide how to split up whatever property and possessions they owned together as a married couple. If one member of the couple is a hoarder and if their home is filled with huge piles

Hoarding behavior can often come to the attention of the authorities. Charles O'Bryan (pictured) is on probation for hoarding-related violations.

of clutter, it can be difficult to decide how to divide the belongings fairly or even how to decide the total worth of the home and everything in it. Simply determining the value of thousands of items in a hoarder's home can be a legal challenge. Unfortunately, whatever debt has been accumulated during a marriage, such as purchases made by credit card, sometimes also must be split evenly between both spouses during a divorce. One spouse may have purchased items on credit cards without telling the other, but both might be equally responsible for paying off the debt, even after a divorce. In this way hoarding can create legal and financial problems for both a hoarder and his or her former spouse.

PRIVATE EYES

"Courts don't like to go onto private property. Living in America, courts have great deference to individual rights and property rights."—Doug Chotkevys, city manager, Dana Point, California

Quoted in Jonathan Volzke and Andrea Swayne. "City Tried for Years to Clean Up Scene of Fatal Fire." *Dana Point (CA) Times*, November 11, 2011. http://danapointtimes .com/view/full_story/16401520/article-City-Tried-for-Years-to-Clean-Up-Scene-of-Fatal -Fire?instance=home_special.

Perhaps the most controversial part of any divorce is the question of who will have custody of the children, if the divorcing couple has any. Deciding which parent the children should live with after a divorce is often where hoarding's consequences become the most visible. The nonhoarding spouse might claim that children are not safe in the hoarder's home because it is unclean, has pest problems, or creates a fire and safety hazard. Courts may order authorities such as housing inspectors and fire department officials to investigate a hoarder's home and decide whether it is safe for children to live there. Sometimes, after a divorce, a hoarder will lose custody of his or her children—not necessarily because he or she is proved not to be a loving, caring parent, but simply because hoarding habits make the home an unsafe place to be.

THE STATE'S RESPONSIBILITY?

"It comes down to civil liberties versus civic responsibility. At what point does the state or government step in?"—Mark Odom, licensed clinical social worker, Orange County, California

Quoted in Jonathan Volzke and Andrea Swayne. "City Tried for Years to Clean Up Scene of Fatal Fire." *Dana Point (CA) Times*, November 11, 2011. http://danapointtimes .com/view/full_story/16401520/article-City-Tried-for-Years-to-Clean-Up-Scene-of-Fatal -Fire?instance=home_special.

Divorce is not the only time when the legal system intervenes in hoarding cases. Sometimes, hoarding behavior comes to the attention of authorities even when the hoarder is secretive about his or her behavior. Neighbors may notice a messy yard or home and complain about it, for example. Cases of animal hoarding are especially noticeable to neighbors because animals make noise and because the smell of animal waste may overwhelm a home and yard. Landlords of rented properties often have concerns about hoarding behavior, too, if they stop by to check on the home and notice that hoarding is occurring. Some hoarders live in apartments or condominiums where their residence shares walls with neighboring residences. Hoarding behavior that creates fire hazards or pest problems in an apartment may put the entire building at risk, since rodents and insects may spread to other units and a fire in one apartment will easily spread to others. There are laws that protect people's right to do what they please within their own home and that forbid authorities like police officers to enter a home without the owner's permission. In cases of hoarding, however, the legal system sometimes gives permission for authorities to enter a home if there is a possible danger to its inhabitants or to neighbors. Many states have laws against animal cruelty, too, and if there is concern that a hoarder owns more animals than the law may allow or that animals are not being kept in a clean and safe environment, the law may intervene.

Children or other dependent relatives can be legally removed from a hoarder's home if police and other agencies decide that

Private Problem, Public Cost

Hoarding typically happens on private property, so police or other officials rarely have the authority to enter a home and force residents to clean out their things. Like anyone else, hoarders have a right to live as they choose within their own home. Unfortunately, though, hoarding can place a financial burden on a community. Illness may force hoarders to move, or a homeowner may pass away and leave a hoarded mess behind. The cost of cleaning out the home then falls either on the person's family or public agencies. Waste haulers, cleaning companies, building inspectors, pest control specialists, animal protection groups, and even building demolishers may have to be hired. Taxpayers sometimes have to pick up the bill for these services. Hoarders' private lifestyle can become a costly public problem, leading some communities to make hoarding a crime. In Orange Village, Ohio, for example, hoarding is a misdemeanor, punishable by up to sixty days in jail. Laws like these are intended to spare a community the potential dangers, hassle, and expense that hoarding can cause, but they are controversial, too. Many people are wary of giving government the power to tell private citizens how much stuff they can own.

Hoarders' private lifestyle can become a costly public problem when outside agencies, like pest control, need to be called in to clean the house.

the living environment is dangerous for them. This is true even in cases where marital divorce and custody battles are not an issue. In extreme cases of hoarding, if authorities investigate and decide that the hoarder caused harm to children, elders, or animals by forcing them to live in dangerous and unsanitary conditions or by neglecting to provide proper care, a hoarder can be sentenced to jail time or forced to pay fines. Hoarders who rent their home from a landlord can also be evicted, or forced to move out, because of hoarding behavior. This can leave a hoarder with nowhere to live.

LIFE, LIBERTY, AND THE PURSUIT OF HAPPINESS

"People can live any way they want as long as it doesn't impact the health and safety of their neighbors or their animals. It's a fine balance between personal property rights and animal cruelty rights. And it's a fine game to get enough probable cause [to legally enter a home]."—Dave Pauli, regional director for the Northern Rockies Regional Office of the Humane Society of the United States

Quoted in Pet-Abuse.com. "Puppy Mill—500 Dogs Seized from Squalor." www.pet -abuse.com/cases/14219/OR/US/#ixzz1fbSkyiIa.

Hoarders may not be able to recognize that their living environment causes safety problems or that they could be doing something illegal. They often argue that their lifestyle is their own choice and they are not harming anyone by living as they choose. Indeed, it is not against the law to live in a messy, cluttered home or to buy and store more items than one truly needs. "Difficult issues of personal freedom, lifestyle choice, and private property rights confound intervening in these cases," say Arluke and Killeen. "Most laws restrict agencies from intervening unless others are being harmed."[45] Many psychologists who work with hoarders agree that these individuals very rarely intend to hurt anybody and may feel blindsided when they are accused of criminal activity. Unfortunately, hoarding sometimes reaches a point at which it *does* break laws, especially when it begins to affect the safety and well-being of a home's human and animal inhabitants. This is why psychologists and other experts on hoarding believe it is important for hoarders and their loved ones to seek help for the problem before it puts their lives in danger or causes them to lose their family or their home.

TREATMENT FOR HOARDING

Hoarding can cause potentially serious health, safety, and legal problems for hoarders and the people who live with them. Unfortunately, because hoarding is still not well understood by the psychology and psychiatry communities, there is still much disagreement about how to treat the behavior effectively. Often, outsiders to the problem—even family members and friends of the person who hoards—argue that the hoarder simply needs to get organized and start throwing things away. People who specialize in working with hoarders often say that the problem is much more complicated than merely being untidy or disorganized. Hoarders usually have deep emotional attachment to their things and find security in being surrounded by their many belongings. Hoarding behavior can be closely tied to one's sense of identity, safety, and happiness, and this separates the condition from being just a problem with clutter and organization. The deeper causes of hoarding are also what make it hard for outsiders to understand and difficult for mental health professionals to treat.

Adding to the problem of effectively treating hoarding is that there is a stigma against hoarders. People seeing the problem for the first time, such as on TV news reports that show the inside of a hoarder's home, might misinterpret hoarding as laziness and think hoarding issues would be easy to solve with trash bags and trips to the town dump. Contrary to what many people may think, however, hoarders tend to be intelligent, well-meaning people, and their behavior usually does not result from laziness or selfishness but from genuine emotion for their belongings. Carrying out a swift disposal of the person's things can therefore be interpreted as a harsh and emotional punishment rather than a helpful gesture.

"Patients have reported feeling a greater sense of attachment to objects than to other people," say David F. Tolin and fellow hoarding researcher Christina M. Gilliam. "Discarding possessions, therefore, is often equated to losing a loved one."[46] This grief-filled outcome is something that hoarders fear when they are considering treatment. Instead of just being urged to throw things away, hoarders usually respond more positively to a kind and gentle approach from professionals who want to help them deal with the thoughts and feelings underlying the hoarding behavior. Whatever the treatment approach, however, the first step in the process of helping a hoarder is for someone to realize that the behavior has reached a point where professional intervention is necessary.

Signs That a Hoarder Needs Help

Recognizing hoarding behavior in the first place can be more difficult than many people realize. Those who hoard tend to be reclusive, often hiding the state of their home even from their closest family members and friends. They may do this at first by confining their clutter to certain rooms or areas of the home, such as a garage or bedroom, and forbidding guests to go into those places. They may keep curtains or window blinds drawn to prevent anyone walking by from peeking in and seeing piles of hoarded items. Usually, a hoarder's clutter problem continues to get worse over time and spills into the main areas of the home, making it impossible to hide from visitors. When this happens, hoarders often insist on meeting friends and family members at locations like parks, restaurants, or other people's homes.

If the hoarder will not invite guests over, it is difficult for friends and family members to see how much or how fast the problem is growing. Especially for those who hoard animals, hoarding can get out of hand very quickly. Dogs and cats that are not neutered or spayed will breed and have puppies and kittens, and if the litters of offspring are kept in the home, the population of animals will increase rapidly. Family members who let many months pass between visits to the hoarder may stop by and find

Hoarders may keep curtains or window blinds drawn to prevent anyone walking by from peeking in and seeing piles of hoarded items.

two dozen animals, whereas at their previous visit there may have been only five or six.

LOWERED VOICES

"No amount of shaming them or yelling at them or having temper tantrums about it is really going to change the issue. It's important for hoarders to realize they're causing other people harm and stress. . . . But hammering away at them for behaving this way is just not helpful."—Judith Kolberg, professional organizer

Quoted in Erin Metcalf. "Hoarding: More than Just a Mess." WebMD, April 2011. www.webmd.com/mental-health/features/harmless-pack-rat-or-compulsive-hoarder.

Even when such a problem is noticed, there may be little that friends or loved ones can do. Hoarders usually do not want friends or family to tell them they have to get rid of their animals or clean out their stuff. Although they may be very aware that their lifestyle is different from other people's, many hoarders do not see it as a problem. They often stubbornly insist that they need all of their things and that their possessions have an important purpose right now or in the future. Recurring arguments tend to occur when hoarders' family members, especially grown children, try to convince hoarders that clutter has overwhelmed them and that they need help. Such arguments can ruin relationships or make hoarders and their loved ones feel emotionally drained and unhappy. "Parents' reaction to interference or complaints about the hoarding ranges from disapproval to emotional abandonment," says psychologist Suzanne A. Chabaud. "Parents emotionally collapse when they feel misunderstood, unloved, and judged." For family members, on the other hand, "psychological pain seems most connected to feeling less valued than the stuff being hoarded,"[47] says Chabaud.

Active Participants in Treatment

Faced with staunch opposition from hoarders, loved ones often feel compelled to reach out for professional help to deal with the behavior. Families may then fear that hoarders will refuse help and turn their back on loved ones because they feel their family has betrayed them. Sometimes, hoarders do admit that they need help to overcome their hoarding, but this often does not happen until they are facing a legal threat or consequence such as divorce, losing custody of their children, or being evicted from their home. In any case effective treatment for hoarding cannot be sought or carried out behind the person's back. Just as hoarders are at the center of the hoarding process, they also need to be at the center of the treatment process.

Agreeing to seek help is a vital first step in the successful treatment of hoarding. Unfortunately, even when hoarders are agreeable, the road to effective behavior change is long. A hoarding problem is usually decades in the making. Piles of hoarded items do not appear overnight, so expecting a home and an entire lifestyle to be transformed overnight is not a reasonable goal, either.

Agreeing to seek help is a vital first step in the successful treatment of hoarding. Jeanne Leier (left) sought the help of friends Nikki Havens (center) and Andria Berke to sort through her hoarded materials.

An Unwanted Inheritance

Children of hoarders are at risk of becoming hoarders themselves, but this is not the only way the burden of hoarding is passed down among generations. Adult children often inherit tons of collected material when a parent who hoards passes away or is forced to move to a nursing home or assisted-living facility. The person's home may be unsafe and unsellable for reasons like dirt, pests, and rotting floorboards. Often, the sheer volume of items stacked and piled from floor to ceiling is overwhelming. In her book about her experiences as the daughter of a compulsive hoarder, Jessie Sholl describes her reaction at the news that she was going to inherit her mother's junk-filled home: "She says it as if she'd be bestowing the most spectacular palace upon me, rather than what her house really is: the source of so many years of frustration, embarrassment, and grief. I can't imagine anything worse than being legally responsible for that house." Though it may be unfair to burden one's adult children with the aftermath of years or decades of hoarding, this is a common outcome and often the source of much disagreement and strife between hoarders and their families.

Jessie Sholl. *Dirty Secret: A Daughter Comes Clean About Her Mother's Compulsive Hoarding.* New York: Gallery, 2011, p. 2.

Hoarders surround themselves with belongings for many different reasons, all of them valid and important to the person. Expecting people to make immediate, sweeping changes to their beliefs and their lifestyle may be unrealistic, so treatment for hoarding usually happens in small stages and over a long period of time.

No Medication for Hoarding

One reason why treatment for hoarding tends to be such a long process is that the thoughts that drive the behavior cannot be lessened immediately just by taking a medication. Hoarding is generally classified as a mental disorder, and because of this, people uninvolved with hoarding might think it is a condition that can be diagnosed and cured by the medical profession. However, there is no pill a person can swallow to get over hoarding quickly and lead an uncluttered life. In fact, this is one of the things that many mental health professionals say distinguishes hoarding from other OCDs. The obsessive thoughts and compulsive behaviors experienced by people who have OCD can often be moderated with medications called selective serotonin reuptake inhibitors (SSRIs), which help brain cells send and receive chemical messages in a way that improves a person's thinking and mood. The compulsions that drive hoarding behavior, however, do not seem to go away if the hoarder takes SSRIs.

Medication can have *some* positive results for hoarders. Studies have shown that more than half of hoarders also suffer from clinical depression. SSRIs do seem to help control severely depressive thoughts and feelings and give hoarders a more positive outlook on life. However, researchers do not know whether depression is what causes hoarding behavior to begin in the first place, or whether the depression is caused by hoarding because the person begins to feel isolated from friends and loved ones. In any case, while controlling depression will certainly help the hoarder face the treatment process with a more positive frame of mind, effective treatment for hoarding is not found within a bottle of pills. Treatment relies instead on the hoarder forming a positive and usually long-term relationship with one or more professionals who specialize in the treatment of hoarding behavior.

Changing Thoughts to Change Behavior

The process psychologists have found to be most successful in treating hoarding behavior is called cognitive-behavioral therapy, or CBT. *Cognition* is the way people think about life, themselves, and the world, so CBT involves making small, gradual changes to a person's way of thinking and the behaviors that result because of it. CBT is believed to be effective for people who hoard because it takes a very individualized approach to the treatment process. Hoarding behavior can begin for many different reasons, all of them unique to the person who hoards. For instance, suffering emotional trauma at some point in life can lead to hoarding behavior, but no two people will have suffered exactly the same trauma and reacted to it in exactly the same way. A therapist working with a client who hoards spends a lot of time talking with the person, trying to figure out what traumatic situations occurred in his or her past and, importantly, how the client responded to them.

Cognitive-behaviorial therapy is believed to be effective for people who hoard because it takes a very individualized approach to the treatment process.

Often, hoarding behavior develops as a coping mechanism, a way to find emotional comfort and feelings of safety and security during or after traumatic events. CBT helps the person decide whether hoarding behavior is tied to his or her need to cope with difficult emotions and memories, and if it is, to begin replacing hoarding with other coping methods that do not have such a negative impact on the person's life. "The clients themselves are not 'sick' or 'abnormal,'" say psychologists Deborah Roth Ledley, Brian P. Marx, and Richard G. Heimberg. "Rather, their problems make a great deal of sense within the context of learned dysfunctional beliefs and behaviors."[48]

STEPPING IN

"The constant refrain we hear from professionals is 'If they aren't a danger to others, then they have a right to live how they want.' When an aging parent runs the daily risk of slipping on glossy magazines on the floor and breaking a hip, or lives in an extreme fire hazard, it's not so easy to stand by and do nothing."—Donna Austin, founder of the Children of Hoarders online support group

Quoted in Deborah Branscum. "The Hoarding Syndrome—When Clutter Goes Out of Control." *Reader's Digest*, March 2007. www.rd.com/health/the-hoarding-syndrome-when -clutter-goes-out-of-control/2.

The chief cause of hoarding is not always a response to some traumatic situation. Sometimes, a compelling need to save everything and be prepared for the future is at the heart of the behavior. Other times, the person becomes very attached to objects he or she possesses, even imagining that they have human-like qualities, and is emotionally distressed by the thought of throwing things away. These and the many other possible causes of hoarding behavior are what a professional therapist helps the person to sort out through CBT. For most therapists, the ultimate goal is to teach hoarders how to help themselves—how to recognize the feelings that make them want to hoard and also how to understand that the behavior they have developed, such as storing thousands of old newspapers, is not reasonable or practical. Through CBT, hoarders can identify thought processes and feelings that make them hoard and also develop more rational behaviors in response to those feelings. "CBT offers hope because it shows how such beliefs and behaviors can be 'unlearned' and how more effective ways of thinking and behaving can be learned,"[49] say Ledley, Marx, and Heimberg.

An Organized Response to Hoarding

CBT is effective therapy for many hoarders because it helps them see where their hoarding behavior is coming from and how it might not be a rational or healthy response to their feelings. Hoarding is a very complex problem for most people, however, and it is not always an emotional problem, at least not in its entirety. To some extent, most hoarders also have problems organizing and sorting items and information. Recognizing the deeper feelings and emotions behind their need to acquire and save things may be helpful, but hoarders may also need professional help with learning how to sort their belongings, throw things away, and create effective organizing systems for the things they do keep.

Specialists in home organization, therefore, have also become a valuable part of the treatment team for many hoarders. Says professional organizer Barbara Savage:

> Compulsive hoarders find that their internal emotional clutter has manifested itself as external clutter. In order to deal with difficult emotional issues, they surround themselves with "things" that are supposed to fill a void or create a cushion of comfort and security. However, too many things around you continually draw your attention in too many directions—keeping a compulsive hoarder from being able to focus and making it hard to ever complete a project or get anything done.[50]

The National Study Group on Chronic Disorganization trains professional organizers specifically to help people who struggle with hoarding tendencies. "These professionals can help you recognize your strengths and capitalize on those to create a structure that will allow you to break free from your need to collect and accumulate,"[51] Savage says.

Building Trust

Whether they are therapists or organizing specialists, one of the biggest challenges professionals face when working with hoarders is building a trusting relationship with the person. Hoarders are inclined to be wary of strangers who come into their homes wanting to help. For most hoarders, past offers of help, such as from family and friends, have included suggestions that the home be cleaned out and sorted through, that animals be given to shelters, or that belongings be thrown away. When others want to throw out their things, most hoarders feel they have lost control of the situation and may refuse to continue treatment. "Anyone working with these patients must remain mindful of the excruciating anxiety they go through at the mere thought—let alone the act—of throwing away their belongings," say psychiatrists Zsuzsa Mezaros and Walter A. Brown. "A cornerstone of management is that the hoarder be the only person who discards his possessions."[52] Thus, an effective treatment relationship begins with establishing trust and reassuring the hoarder that things will not be tossed out without his or her permission. Professionals who work with hoarders spend a lot of time getting to the know them and usually make many visits to the person's home, since treatment has been found to be most effective when it is based on trust and takes place within the hoarder's own environment.

Home visits can create additional challenges for those who want to help treat hoarding, though. The homes of some hoarders may be not just untidy but unsanitary as well. Thick dust, decomposing food, towers of clutter, and possible infestations of insects or rodents can make it difficult to spend time in a hoarder's home. Animal hoarders may have the most unpleasant environments of all—the strong odors created by the urine and feces of many animals living in a small space can be hard to withstand. Professionals who treat hoarding behavior must be prepared to visit even the dirtiest of homes without being judgmental. Hoarders are often embarrassed by their homes already, and sensing that the person who is coming by to help them is disgusted by their lifestyle could make hoarders unwilling to move forward with the treatment process. Hoarding behavior, however, does

Building trust with a hoarder is an essential part of his or her recovery. Jim Curlee (left) has a trusting relationship with his professional organizer Wendy Taddeucci.

not automatically mean that a person lives in squalor—a condition of being unclean to the extent of being unhealthy. "In fact," say Christiana Bratiotis, Cristina Sorrentino Schmalisch, and Gail Steketee, "squalid home conditions have been relatively rare among hoarding participants in our research studies."[53] Whatever the state of the person's home, though, facing the accumulated clutter in a straightforward, nonjudgmental way could make the difference between a successful hoarding intervention or an attempt that is doomed to fail.

Professional therapists generally agree that to treat hoarding effectively, the client has to be the one making choices about what needs to be kept and what can be thrown away, and also how best to go about this process. In most hoarding cases only when hoarders feel in complete control of their own belongings and the decisions being made about these items will they effectively be able to take steps toward eliminating and sorting their own clutter. Professionals who deal with hoarding also realize that they need to set realistic goals for treatment. The hoarder may never be able to live in a completely uncluttered and perfectly organized environment. The best outcome to be hoped for might only be that the hoarder can control piles of clutter enough that the home can be cleaned and the safety of inhabitants is not compromised. "Treatment takes time and clients may not be recovered . . . at the end of the intervention," say Gail Steketee and Randy O. Frost, "but most experience significant reduction in clutter, difficulty discarding, and excessive acquiring."[54] Even getting to this point can be a long and difficult process, however. Those who hoard usually face an ongoing struggle with this difficult problem.

Treatment Is Lifelong and Costly

Some people, even some hoarders themselves, argue that therapy for hoarding should be swift—simply clean out the mess and start fresh. TV shows about hoarders sometimes make it seem like this is a realistic goal, since by the end of many episodes, the featured hoarder's home has been cleaned out and he or she seems content and relieved. The viewing public gets the idea that hoarding could be fixed in one weekend with a dumpster and a few good friends willing to help remove the mess. Unfortunately, follow-up television episodes rarely show the reality of hoarding—that even when the original hoard is cleaned out, more clutter often begins to creep in, or the person starts to acquire new pets once again. "Many of our clients have experienced forced 'clean-outs' by authorities or relatives," say Steketee and Frost. "Their strong angry or hurt reactions and continuing struggle with hoarding indicate that this is not an effective alternative."[55]

Contrary to what TV shows often suggest, treatment for hoarding is almost never accomplished in a single weekend. The struggle to resist hoarding urges is usually a lifelong process, and treatment may take months or even years before the hoarder reaches a point of feeling able to control the need to acquire things, overcome resistance to throwing things away, and organize the belongings he or she does keep. Unfortunately, such ongoing treatment for hoarding is costly, and many hoarders are unable to afford treatment for the full length of time that would be most beneficial. Instead, many hoarders receive treatment in spurts, and in between treatment periods, they may sink back into their old hoarding habits. "Motivation can fluctuate over time," say Jamie Feusner and Sanjaya Saxena, psychiatrists specializing in hoarding and anxiety-related disorders. "Patients usually must work tremendously hard to adhere to treatment."[56]

THE PATH NOT TAKEN

"Those struggling with hoarding often try unsuccessfully to get control but are chronically overwhelmed. . . . They can't make decisions because decisions always involve the loss of the choice not made."—Suzanne B. Phillips, licensed psychologist

Suzanne B. Phillips. "Hoarding Behavior: Another Perspective." *Healing Together for Couples* (blog), Psych Central. http://blogs.psychcentral.com/healing-together/2011/06/hoarding -behavior-another-perspective.

Hoarding can be a frustrating, long-term problem, not just for the hoarder but for his or her loved ones, who may feel they cannot do any more to help. One thing that makes hoarding so difficult to overcome is that by the time anyone usually seeks treatment for it, the hoarding has already gone on for years or even decades. Habits that take a lifetime to form might seem to take another lifetime to break. This is why increased public awareness of hoarding in recent years, even if it comes through TV shows that might portray hoarding and its treatment unrealistically, could actually help hoarders in the long run. As more people become aware of hoarding, they may also recognize early signs of the behavior in themselves or in their loved ones and take action to correct hoarding before it gets out of control.

Early Identification for Hoarders

Those who work with compulsive hoarders have found that identifying hoarding tendencies early in a person's life greatly increases the chances that the person will lead a normal life and not become overly encumbered by animals or possessions. Since hoarding behavior, for most people, begins in childhood and tends to run in families, parents themselves may play an important role in halting what might become a hoarding cycle. If they have a tendency to hoard and they receive help for the problem while their children still live at home, parents can begin to help kids and teens identify what hoarding behavior involves and how to deal positively with the urge to collect things and the dread of throwing things away. Hoarding, for most children and teenagers, is a mild situation that does not yet interfere with their quality of life. Helping them to think logically about possessions from an early age could keep hoarding from ever becoming a problem that could endanger their health, affect their personal relationships, and put them at risk of losing their home.

Some experts caution that public awareness of hoarding behavior has made people see and fear hoarding situations even when there are none, however. An untidy, disorganized person is not necessarily a hoarder, and a hoarder is not necessarily untidy or messy, either. To effectively recognize hoarding problems, people ultimately must look past the mess of the hoard and look to the person that lives in the mess. It is unproductive to label hoarders as lazy, slovenly, or selfish. It is also unhelpful to assume that there is an easy fix for their problems. If society begins

A Lifelong Habit

Hoarding manifests as a lifelong pattern of accumulating things, and the effects of hoarding usually get more pronounced with time. An older hoarder who has been storing items in her home for decades is even more likely to live in a severely overcrowded and unsafe environment than is a younger hoarder who has not yet accumulated possessions for quite as long. Unfortunately, elderly hoarders' age also puts them at a greater risk of injury if they trip and fall or become trapped beneath a collapsed pile of clutter. They are also more likely to feel isolated, lonely, and depressed. Advanced age alone raises the risk of isolation and depression, and hoarding may only compound the situation. Problematic though hoarding can be for elders, helping them to change their hoarding habits is also especially difficult. The lifestyle of elderly hoarders may have been unchanged for decades, and hoarders may feel that their possessions are the most important things left in their life. Sometimes it is necessary to remove an elderly hoarders' belongings or even for them to move out of their home because of health complications due to age. These outcomes, which would be emotionally trying for any hoarder, are especially difficult for someone who is also elderly.

An older hoarder who has been storing items for decades is even more likely to live in a severely overcrowded and unsafe environment like the one pictured in which an elderly couple was buried alive.

to better understand hoarding as a behavior that stems from fears and worries or from a different way of viewing one's life and possessions, people may be in a better position to help hoarders by showing them compassion and support. Judgment and misunderstanding often serve only to isolate hoarders even further and worsen their hoarding habits. Statistically, most people know someone who hoards. An increased awareness and understanding of the disorder could help more people reach out to hoarders, possibly stopping this from being a hidden problem so often suffered in isolation and embarrassment.

NOTES

Introduction: Behind Closed Doors: The Hidden Problem of Hoarding

1. Quoted in Michael Morton. "Bellingham Couple Died Amid Clutter." *MetroWest Daily News* (Framingham, MA), July 17, 2010. www.metrowestdailynews.com/features/x242417496/Couple-died-amid-clutter#ixzz1ffNtKM5Y.

Chapter 1: Hoarding Behavior, Past to Present

2. William Bryk. "The Collyer Brothers: Past & Present." *New York Sun*, April 13, 2005. www.nysun.com/on-the-town/collyer-brothers/12165.

3. Quoted in Everyday Health. "Does Reality TV Accurately Portray Hoarding?" www.everydayhealth.com/anxiety-disorders/experts-does-tv-accurately-portray-hoarding.aspx.

4. Quoted in Everyday Health. "Does Reality TV Accurately Portray Hoarding?"

5. Quoted in Everyday Health. "Does Reality TV Accurately Portray Hoarding?"

6. Quoted in Everyday Health. "Does Reality TV Accurately Portray Hoarding?"

7. Quoted in Dan Stamm. "Iguanas, Alligators, More Found in South Philly Home." NBC Philadelphia, Wednesday, July 27, 2011. www.nbcphiladelphia.com/news/breaking/Shunk-South-Philly-Iguana-Dead-Dogs-126217388.html.

8. Arnold Arluke, et al. "Press Reports of Animal Hoarding." *Society & Animals*, 2002. www.animalsandsociety.org/assets/library/454_s1021.pdf.

9. Arnold Arluke, et al. "Press Reports of Animal Hoarding."

Chapter 2: Hoarding as a Disorder

10. Max Taylor and Ethel Quayle. *Child Pornography: An Internet Crime*. New York: Brunner-Routledge, 2005, p. 149.

11. Taylor and Quayle. *Child Pornography*, p. 149.

12. Bruce M. Hyman and Cherry Pedrick. *The OCD Workbook: Your Guide to Breaking Free from Obsessive-Compulsive Disorder*. Oakland, CA: New Harbinger, 2010, p. 233.

13. Michael A. Tompkins and Tamara L. Hartl. *Digging Out: Helping Your Loved One Manage Clutter, Hoarding, and Compulsive Acquiring*, Oakland, CA: New Harbinger, 2009, p. 15.

14. Randy O. Frost and Gail Steketee. *Stuff: Compulsive Hoarding and the Meaning of Things*. New York: Houghton Mifflin Harcourt, 2010, p. 14.

15. Cheryl Carmin. *Obsessive-Compulsive Disorder Demystified: An Essential Guide for Understanding and Living with OCD*. Cambridge, MA: Da Capo, 2009, p. 54.

16. Edna B. Foa. *Mastery of Obsessive-Compulsive Disorder*. New York: Oxford University Press, 2004, p. 65.

17. Christiana Bratiotis, Cristina Sorrentino Schmalisch, and Gail Steketee. *The Hoarding Handbook: A Guide for Human Service Professionals*. New York: Oxford University Press, 2011, pp. 58–59.

18. David F. Tolin, Randy O. Frost, and Gail Steketee. *Buried in Treasures: Help for Acquiring, Saving, and Hoarding*. New York: Oxford University Press, 2007, p. 102.

19. Bratiotis, Schmalisch, and Steketee. *The Hoarding Handbook*, p. 9.

Chapter 3: Why People Hoard

20. Quoted in Alexandria Abramian-Mott. "They're Not Hoarders, They're Just Messy." *Los Angeles Times*, January 29, 2011. http://articles.latimes.com/2011/jan/29/home/la-hm-kid hoard-20110129.

21. Arnold Arluke and Celeste Killeen. *Inside Animal Hoarding: The Case of Barbara Erickson and Her 552 Dogs*. West Lafayette, IN: Purdue University Press, 2009, p. 174.

22. Frost and Steketee. *Stuff*, p. 93.

23. Frost and Steketee. *Stuff*, p. 92.

24. Tolin, Frost, and Steketee. *Buried in Treasures*, p. 105.

25. Tolin, Frost, and Steketee. *Buried in Treasures*, p. 105.

26. Tolin, Frost, and Steketee. *Buried in Treasures*, p. 102.

27. Jon Hershfield. "Memory Hoarding in Obsessive Compulsive Disorder (OCD)." *Obsessive-Compulsive Disorder* (blog), OCD Center of Los Angeles, July 14, 2010. www.ocdla.com /blog/memory-hoarding-obsessive-compulsive-disorder-ocd -886.

28. Tolin, Frost, and Steketee. *Buried in Treasures*, p. 102.

29. Quoted in Peter Walsh. "Clutter Genetics." Oprah.com, June 8, 2007. www.oprah.com/oprahradio/clutter-Genetics.

30. Quoted in Abramian-Mott. "They're Not Hoarders, They're Just Messy."

31. Quoted in Frank R. Ascione, ed. *The International Handbook of Animal Abuse and Cruelty*. West Lafayette, IN: Purdue University Press, 2009, p. 228.

Chapter 4: The Hidden Costs of Hoarding

32. Bratiotis, Schmalisch, and Steketee. *Hoarding Handbook*, p. 59.

33. Tompkins and Hartl. *Digging Out*, p. 15.

34. Fugen Neziroglu, Jill Slaven, and Katharine Donnelly. "How Compulsive Hoarding Affects Families." International OCD Foundation. www.ocfoundation.org/hoarding/family.aspx# affects_families.

35. Neziroglu, Slaven, and Donnelly. "How Compulsive Hoarding Affects Families."

36. Neziroglu, Slaven, and Donnelly. "How Compulsive Hoarding Affects Families."

37. Neziroglu, Slaven, and Donnelly. "How Compulsive Hoarding Affects Families."

38. Carmin. *Obsessive-Compulsive Disorder Demystified*, pp. 56–57.

39. Cheryl Mendelson. *Home Comforts: The Art and Science of Keeping House*. New York: Scribner, 1999, p. 456.

40. Arluke and Killeen. *Inside Animal Hoarding*, p. 1.

41. Quoted in Kristine Harrington. "Hoarding Creates New Dangers to Firefighters." Idaho Fire Chiefs Association, March 23, 2011. www.idahofirechiefs.org/default.asp?deptid=1&com=news&pressID=1895.

42. Beth Ann McNeill. *Emergency Care and Transportation of the Sick and Injured: Case Studies.* Burlington, MA: Jones & Bartlett Learning, 2012, p. 199.

43. McNeill. *Emergency Care and Transportation of the Sick and Injured*, p. 199.

44. Quoted in Steven Kurutz. "Children of Hoarders on Leaving the Nest." *New York Times*, May 11, 2011. www.nytimes.com/2011/05/12/garden/children-of-hoarders-on-leaving-the-cluttered-nest.html?pagewanted=all.

45. Arluke and Killeen. *Inside Animal Hoarding*, p. 179.

Chapter 5: Treatment for Hoarding

46. Quoted in Robert Hudak and Darin Dougherty, eds. *Clinical Obsessive-Compulsive Disorders in Adults and Children.* Cambridge: Cambridge University Press, 2011, p. 129.

47. Suzanne A. Chabaud. "The Hidden Lives of Children of Hoarders." *Psychiatric Times*, November 10, 2011. www.psychiatrictimes.com/ocd/content/article/10168/1989161.

48. Deborah Roth Ledley, Brian P. Marx, and Richard G. Heimberg. *Making Cognitive Behavioral Therapy Work: Clinical Process for New Practitioners.* 2nd ed. New York: Guilford, 2010, p. 3.

49. Ledley, Marx, and Heimberg. *Making Cognitive Behavioral Therapy Work*, pp. 3–4.

50. Barbara Savage. "Compulsive Hoarding." *Get Organized*, February 2006. www.onlineorganizing.com/NewslettersArticle.asp?article=511&newsletter=go.

51. Savage. "Compulsive Hoarding."

52. Zsuzsa Mezaros and Walter A. Brown. "The Perils of Hoarding and How to Intervene." *Psychiatric Times*, May 31, 2006. www.psychiatrictimes.com/display/article/10168/56226.

53. Bratiotis, Schmalisch, and Steketee. *Hoarding Handbook*, p. 11.

54. Steketee and Frost. *Compulsive Hoarding*, p. 16.

55. Steketee and Frost. *Compulsive Hoarding*, p. 16.
56. Jamie Feusner and Sanjaya Saxena. "Compulsive Hoarding: Unclutter Lives and Homes by Breaking Anxiety's Grip." *Journal of Family Practice*, March 2005. www.jfponline.com /Pages.asp?AID=458.

Chapter 1: Hoarding Behavior, Past to Present

1. The author says several decades passed after the incident with the Collyer brothers' New York City home before scientists started studying hoarding seriously. Why do you think it took the scientific community so long to become interested in hoarding?

2. Do you think reality TV shows do a service by exposing hoarding behavior, or do you think they exploit hoarders' living situations? Explain your answer.

3. Is it fair for the media to call hoarding "extremely bizarre" or "criminal" behavior? Why or why not?

Chapter 2: Hoarding as a Disorder

1. Hoarding researchers Randy Frost and Gail Steketee are quoted as saying that collecting, procrastination, and holding on to sentimental keepsakes are all "part of the hoarding story." What do you think this means? How are hoarders both similar to and different from people who collect, procrastinate on their cleaning, or keep memorabilia?

2. In what ways is hoarding behavior like a compulsion to avoid something negative and also like an addiction to seek something positive?

3. Do you believe that hoarding is a psychological disorder? Give a few details from this chapter to support your answer.

Chapter 3: Why People Hoard

1. According to what you read in this chapter, what are some differences between the way most hoarders organize compared with organizing strategies of most people who do not hoard?

2. The author says that hoarding runs strongly in families and that it may be genetic, a learned behavior, or both. What are

advantages and disadvantages of calling hoarding a genetic condition? Similarly, what are advantages and disadvantages of calling it a learned behavior?

3. What does it mean to anthropomorphize an object or animal? What role do you think anthropomorphizing might have in hoarders' habit of keeping so many things?

Chapter 4: The Hidden Costs of Hoarding

1. The author mentions several ways that hoarding behavior can cost someone in terms of money, health, and safety. Which of these possible costs do you think is the most serious consequence of hoarding, and why?

2. How does the author say that hoarding behavior can affect children? At what point, if ever, do you think children should be forced to move out of a hoarder's home?

3. Do you think legal authorities should be allowed to enter a hoarder's home and force the person to change his or her lifestyle? Or do you think people should always be allowed to do what they want in their own home? Give examples or details to support your opinion.

Chapter 5: Treatment for Hoarding

1. The author says that hoarding behavior is linked to clinical depression. Do you think the effects of hoarding, such as isolation, cause depression? Or do you think depression instead causes people to start hoarding? Explain or support your answer.

2. Based on what you read in this chapter, why do you think that merely throwing out a hoarder's accumulated belongings usually does not "cure" the behavior?

3. Do you think that someone you know might have early signs of hoarding behavior? What are some things you could suggest that the person do to keep the behavior from getting out of control?

ORGANIZATIONS TO CONTACT

American Psychological Association (APA)
750 First St. NE
Washington, DC 20002-4242
Phone: (800) 374-2721
Website: www.apa.org

The APA is a scientific and professional organization that represents psychologists in the United States and is the largest association of psychologists worldwide. Its mission is to advance psychological knowledge to benefit society and improve people's lives. Its searchable website contains information on many psychological conditions, including compulsive behaviors like hoarding.

American Society for the Prevention of Cruelty to Animals (ASPCA)
424 E. Ninety-Second St.
New York, NY 10128-6804
Phone: (888) 666-2279
Website: www.aspca.org

The ASPCA was founded in 1866 as a humane organization in the Western Hemisphere whose mission is to rescue animals from abuse, advocate for humane treatment of animals, and share resources with animal shelters nationwide. The ASPCA's website also has information on animal hoarding, its causes, and what can be done to help hoarders.

Children of Hoarders
Website: http://childrenofhoarders.com

Children of Hoarders is a not-for profit organization that aims to increase awareness and understanding of hoarding behavior as experienced by children of hoarders. It provides resources and a supportive community of peers for those whose parents have problems with hoarding.

Institute for Challenging Disorganization
1693 S. Hanley Rd.
St. Louis, MO 63144
Phone: (314) 416-2236
Website: www.challengingdisorganization.org
E-mail: icd@challengingdisorganization.org

This organization aims to help people with what it terms chronic disorganization, which may be a precursor to full-blown hoarding behavior. Its website offers fact sheets and other resources for learning more about disorganization and hoarding.

International OCD Foundation (IOCDF)
PO Box 961029
Boston, MA 02196
Phone: (617) 973-5801
Fax: (617) 973-5803
E-mail: info@ocfoundation.org
Website: www.ocfoundation.org

The IOCDF is an international not-for-profit organization of people with OCD and related disorders, as well as their families, friends, professionals, and others. It aims to raise awareness of OCD and related disorders, improve treatment options, support research, make information accessible for those with OCD and related disorders, and lobby for the OCD community. The IOCDF has a special center focused on hoarding.

National Association of Professional Organizers
15000 Commerce Pkwy., Suite C
Mount Laurel, NJ 08054
Phone: (856) 380-6828
Fax: (856) 439-0525
E-mail: napo@napo.net
Website: www.napo.net

The goal of this group of more than four thousand professional organizers is to help individuals bring order and efficiency to their lives by conquering clutter and chaos. The organization offers advice and insight on organizing as well as a way to connect those who hoard with professional organizers who might help them.

FOR MORE INFORMATION

Books

Judith Kolberg. *What Every Professional Organizer Needs to Know About Hoarding.* Decatur, GA: Squall, 2009. The founder of the National Study Group on Chronic Disorganization discusses the psychological challenges and difficulty with organization that affect hoarders. This book explains hoarding from an organizational viewpoint and suggests a variety of approaches for helping a person who hoards.

Matt Paxton and Phaedra Hise. *The Secret Lives of Hoarders: True Stories of Tackling Extreme Clutter.* New York: Perigee Trade, 2011. Written by a hoarding therapist who has helped hundreds of clients with the disorder, this book gives multiple accounts of severe hoarding cases, focusing on what makes people hoard, how to recognize signs of the behavior before it gets severe, and how hoarders, their friends, and their loved ones can cope.

David F. Tolin, Randy O. Frost, and Gail Steketee. *Buried in Treasures.* New York: Oxford University Press, 2007. Written by psychologists who study hoarding behavior, this book explains hoarding causes and some things people who are concerned about hoarding behavior can do to help themselves.

Robin Zasio. *The Hoarder in You: How to Live a Happier, Healthier, Uncluttered Life.* Emmaus, PA: Rodale, 2011. Written by a hoarding therapist, this book explains compulsive hoarding in terms of impulses most people have, such as emotional attachment to belongings or enjoyment of collecting things. It also discusses what everyone can learn about acquiring and saving by studying extreme hoarding cases.

Internet Sources

Oprah.com. "Hoarding Resources." July 18, 2008. www.oprah.com /home/How-to-Stop-Hoarding-Resources. This article explains causes and symptoms of hoarding, discusses whether it can be treated, and contains a self-assessment for whether someone has a hoarding problem.

Kayla Webley. "Hoarding: How Collecting Stuff Can Control Your Life." *Time*, April 26, 2010. www.time.com/time/nation/article /0,8599,1984444,00.html. This article features an interview with psychologists and hoarding experts Randy O. Frost and Gail Steketee that explores hoarding behavior and its causes.

Websites

Hoarders, A&E (www.aetv.com/hoarders). This companion website to A&E's television show *Hoarders* offers links to select episodes.

Hoarding: Buried Alive (tlc.howstuffworks.com/tv/hoarding -buried-alive). TLC's popular reality television show about hoarding maintains this site with information about hoarding and links to parts of its episodes featuring cases of extreme hoarding.

INDEX

PICTURE CREDITS

Cover: © MCarper/shutterstock.com
© ALEX GARCIA/MCT/Landov, 66, 92
© ANDREW A. NELLES/MCT/Landov, 53
© AP Images/Al Behrman, 70
© AP Images/Brad McClenny, 19
© AP Images/John Mahoney, 17
© AP Photo/Santiago Flores, South Bend Tribune, 88
© Edward Jackson/NY Daily News Archive/Getty Images, 11
© Eight Arts Photography/Alamy, 25
© Finnbarr Webster/Alamy, 56
© Gale/Cengage Learning, 27, 45
© Janine Wiedel Photolibrary/Alamy, 29
© Jim West/Alamy, 42–43
© JOEL KOYAMA/MCT/Landov, 80-81
© Juniors Bildarchiv/Alamy, 38
© Kumar Sriskandan/Alamy, 41
© LAR Lifestyle/Alamy, 32
© Marmaduke St. John/Alamy, 59
© PhotoStock-Israel/Alamy, 84
© Portrait Essentials/Alamy, 22
© Powered by Light/Alan Spencer/Alamy, 73
© Realimage/Alamy, 63
© Richard Levine/Alamy, 7
© Sandy Huffaker/Corbis, 21
© shinypix/Alamy, 48
© Sylvia Serrado/Workbook Stock/Getty Images, 36
© Tom Joslyn/Alamy, 78

ABOUT THE AUTHOR

Jenny MacKay is the author of fifteen nonfiction books for kids and teens on topics ranging from crime scene investigation to social issues. She lives in northern Nevada with her husband and two children.